The Second Book of Experiments

Everyday life is full of science. Cleaning,
washing, cooking, using a radio or TV,
taking photographs, making music,
travelling by car or train – all these involve
practising or using science. You can't
understand how these things work – or
repair them – without a basic knowledge of
science. There are plenty of possibilities
at home to penetrate into the secrets and
mysteries of nature – by experiments.

Some most amazing scientific experiments
can be performed with simple, everyday
things found in almost every household.
Experiments with heat, gases, liquids, sound
and astronomy.

3 bcd

Also by Leonard de Vries

THE BOOK OF EXPERIMENTS

and published by Carousel Books

LEONARD DE VRIES

THE SECOND
BOOK OF EXPERIMENTS

Translated by Eric G. Breeze

Illustrated by Joost van de Woestijne

CAROUSEL EDITOR: ANNE WOOD

CAROUSEL BOOKS
A DIVISION OF TRANSWORLD PUBLISHERS LTD
A NATIONAL GENERAL COMPANY

THE SECOND BOOK OF EXPERIMENTS
A CAROUSEL BOOK 0 552 54032 3

Originally published in Great Britain
by John Murray

PRINTING HISTORY
John Murray edition published 1963
John Murray edition reprinted 1964
John Murray edition reprinted 1968
Carousel edition published 1973
Reprinted 1974

Carousel Books are published by
Transworld Publishers Ltd., Cavendish House,
57-59 Uxbridge Road, Ealing, London W.5 5SA

Printed by James Paton Ltd.,
Paisley, Scotland

Contents

EXPERIMENTS WITH FORCES

1. To err is human 7
2. Challenge to weightlifters 8
3. Ten against one – how strong you are! 9
4. Stand up . . . it's impossible! 10
5. Paper is stronger than you think 11
6. A bridge of . . . paper 12
7. Make your own seconds pendulum 13
8. It happens on the dot 14
9. The immovable tower 16
10. Which will you break? The hairs or the stick? 17
11. Where does the coin fall? 18
12. The wandering coin 19
13. A flywheel from a button 20
14. Your jet engine runs on . . . water 22
15. Acrobatic forks 23
16. What a complicated equilibrium! 24
17. The marvel of centrifugal force 25
18. Ounce, lift up a pound 27

EXPERIMENTS ON SOUND

19. John speaking to Margaret is a rather complicated affair 29
20. Make your own xylophone 40
21. How to make a Swanee whistle 43
22. A string bass from a box and a piece of string 45
23. Listen to the beat of your heart 47
24. And the bottle said 'Boo!' 48
25. Thanks to resonance 50
26. Make a model of sound waves 52
27. Reflection of sound 54
28. Sound + sound = silence 56
29. High plus higher can be low 57
30. What causes the Doppler effect? 59
31. A gun for sound rings 61

EXPERIMENTS WITH GASES

32. A fountain in a glass case 64
33. The balloon and the bottle 65
34. From walking tumblers to Hovercraft 66

5

35. Waterdrops . . . skaters 67
36. Blow a flame towards you 69
37. Air resistance as a life saver 71
38. Fly a 'slow roll' 72
39. Make your own gasworks 73
40. Aeroplane wing . . . fly! 74

EXPERIMENTS WITH LIQUIDS

41. The wonderful story of a drop of water 76
42. A waterpipe from . . . wool or cotton threads 83
43. The drop of a coin 85
44. Capillarity again 86
45. Make a siphon 87
46. Which hole will win? 88
47. A water scale 89
48. Oil and vinegar from the same bottle 90
49. A liquid tricolour 92
50. Waterproof bandage? 93
51. A sea change 95
52. The strange antics of a table tennis ball 95

EXPERIMENTS ON HEAT

53. Expansion by heat 97
54. Make a thermometer 98
55. A sawdust roundabout 99
56. Why is this candle hollow? 101
57. Cooling by evaporation 101

58. Colder with soda and hypo 103
59. Make your own ice-cream 104
60. Make your own clouds and snowstorm 105
61. Soap bubbles of . . . crystals 107
62. Right through the ice, but the ice stays whole 108
63. Does ice melt in boiling water? 110
64. Make a steam turbine 111
65. Pick the right coin every time 112

EXPERIMENTS ON ASTRONOMY

66. Between you and infinity there are billions of stars 114
67. Make a model of the expanding universe 123
68. A spiral nebula from . . . tea-leaves 124
69. Make your own eclipse of the sun and moon 125
70. Make an astronomical telescope 127
71. Bring the moon, planets and stars nearer 129
72. See sunspots 132
73. Make a sundial 133
74. Where is the south? 134
75. Foucault's pendulum 136
76. The spinning earth 137

A letter from the author 139

1. To err is human

You will need: 2 tins the same size, sand, gravel or nails.

When we lift something up we estimate its weight beforehand and according to our estimate we prepare our muscles for the effort they must make. Normally we do this without thinking, quite unconsciously – but it can lead to some amusing mistakes.

Take two tins, exactly alike, and fill one with something heavy like sand, gravel or nails, and put the lids on both of them. Set the full and the empty tin side by side on a table and ask someone, without telling him the difference, to raise them both at the same time to the same height (about 2 feet) on a signal from you. This looks very simple, and your friend will be quite sure

7

that he can do it. 'Nothing in it,' he says. Now clap your hands or shout 'NOW!' You can be certain that the hand with the empty tin will shoot up much higher than the other hand which may hardly rise at all! You can do the same experiment with two equally sized cases standing on the ground, one well filled and the other empty.

At a circus once I saw one of those mighty strong men with bulging muscles give an impressive demonstration of weight lifting. The iron bar, with its black metal discs at the ends, looked so heavy that I thought I would not even be able to raise it off the ground. But the strong man, with a great show of muscle power, lifted it right above his head to a tremendous round of applause from the audience. When the weightlifter had finished his act and walked off the heavy thing was left lying in the ring and we wondered how many men would be needed to carry it away. We were struck speechless when, a little later, a small clown came in, picked it up with two fingers and ran off with it, grinning all over his face. We had been well and truly fooled. Yes, to err is human.

2. Challenge to weightlifters

You will need: heavy book, piece of strong string, boy who thinks that he is very tough.

For this astounding experiment you must seek out the strongest of your friends – a real weightlifter! Get a very heavy book and tie round it a piece of strong string about 5 feet long. Now ask your friend the weightlifter to take hold of an end of the string in each hand

and then pull as hard as he can so that the two halves of the string form one horizontal line.

No matter how strong your tough friend is, he will find it quite impossible to pull the string out straight. But it's not his fault. It is the fault of the laws of nature. The greater the angle between the two halves of the string the greater the force which must be exerted to hold the book up. And the nearer this angle approaches to 180°, the greater is the increase of the force which is required. Your mighty friend is more likely to break the string than get the two halves in one line!

3. Ten against one – how strong you are!
You will need: some people, wall.

'Two against one, that's not fair!' Why? Because, in general, two people are stronger than one. Then surely *ten* against one is even more unfair.

Now look at the drawing. That's ten against one, isn't it? How is it possible then? Have a try. The 'one' is you. Place your hands on the wall and take a firm stand. Get several people to stand behind you – people about as strong as yourself. Each pushes against the person in front, and together they push you – or so it seems, because, to everyone's astonishment, you hold them all!

9

What is the secret? Simply this: no person can pass on more force than he can exert himself – otherwise he would collapse! All along the line each person braces himself against the push from behind by pushing in front. He may, if he's stronger, push harder than the person behind, but it's only *his* push that affects the next one. So all you have to worry about is the person immediately behind *you*. If you can hold him you can hold ten, twenty, a hundred – a thousand! Try it in stages with as many friends as you can get together.

4. Stand up . . . it's impossible!

You will need: plain chair with an upright back, yourself.

Sit on a chair just like the boy in the picture, with your back straight and placed right up against the back of the chair. Your legs should be vertical and your feet flat on the floor. Do you think it is possible to get up from this position? This means that you must not alter your position in any way before you rise, you must not bend your body nor move your feet.

But even though you try with every ounce of will and energy that you can muster, you cannot do it. However, if you bend forward so that the upper part of your body comes above your feet, or if you move your feet far enough back beneath the upper part of your body, then you can stand up – and there's no other way to do it.

If you find the construction of a motor-car complicated, remember that the construction of the human body is a thousand times more complicated and that, for example, the muscular system is a marvel of technology and applied mechanics. The simple act of sitting down and getting up again involves teamwork of muscles and forces of a complexity unequalled in the realm of technology.

5. Paper is stronger than you think

You will need: a few sheets of paper, elastic band, some books.

From an ordinary sheet of writing paper you can make a pillar which can support a load of several pounds, incredible though it may sound. But we are going to prove it experimentally.

Roll the paper into a cylinder with a diameter of about 2 inches, and hold it together with an elastic band. Now on top of the paper pillar lay a heavy book – take care that it does not fall over – then another book, and another book, and another. . . .

If you put the succeeding books on very carefully you will find out just how strong your rolled-up paper is, for it can bear a load of many pounds with ease. Carry on piling on the books and the moment comes when the pillar gives way. Take notice of the peculiarly formed creases which appear in the paper. Find out across which diameter the pillar is strongest.

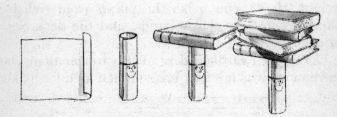

Hollow tubes combine great strength with light weight and consequently find many applications both in nature and in technology. Hence most of our bones are hollow as anyone who has dug the marrow out of a marrowbone will know. Hollow steel tubes are used a very great deal for scaffolding and other structures.

6. A bridge of . . . paper

You will need: 3 empty jars, sheet of paper.

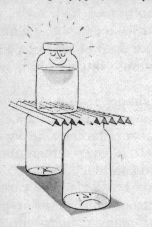

It seems an impossible idea: to make a bridge of paper between two jam jars strong enough to support a third jar. Rolling the paper as in the previous experiment will not do here. But there are other ways of making paper strong. For example, folding, or pleating. Fold the paper as is shown in the picture, lay it across the two jam jars and the limp piece of paper will be able to support the third jam jar.

By combining this experiment and the preceding one you can make a bridge entirely of paper, on hollow piers, which will be able to support a considerable weight. How? You make the pillars from rolled-up paper secured by elastic bands, and the deck of the bridge from pleated paper.

Corrugated cardboard is much stronger than plain cardboard, which is why it is so much used for making

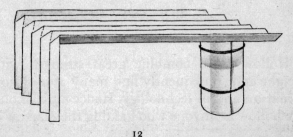

boxes. A variation on this is corrugated iron, which is often used as a roofing material: it is very strong and at the same time provides channels for the rain to run off easily. In the construction of aeroplanes, in which great strength and lightness of weight are so important, considerable use is made of tubes and corrugated sheets. Floors are made like honeycombs. Think for yourself where in nature or technology you come across similar strong but light structures.

7. Make your own seconds pendulum

You will need: clock or watch with seconds hand, some thread, small weight, tape measure.

It is very interesting to make a pendulum which swings to and fro in exactly 1 second each way. You will need a piece of thread with a loop at one end so that it can be hung from a nail, and a weight at the other. The thread (including the loop and the weight) must be about 33 inches long. For a weight you can use some small, heavy object like a metal nut or a pebble.

The pendulum must be free to swing, so that neither the thread nor the weight touches anything. If the pendulum is exactly the right length one double swing there and back (known as the 'period') will take precisely 2 seconds. (Although this takes 2 seconds, it is still known as a seconds pendulum from the time of a single swing.) How can you ensure that the time of the swing, there or back, is exactly 1 second?

You can do this best with a clock or watch which has a seconds hand. Let the pendulum make 60 single swings, i.e. 30 double swings – it is merely a question of counting – and see if they take 60 seconds. It will be sheer chance if you get it right first time. If the 60 swings take more than 60 seconds, shorten the thread a little, while if they take less, lengthen it. Remember to start the pendulum from roughly the same position each time.

When you have succeeded in making your pendulum with a period of exactly 2 seconds perhaps you would like to investigate what effect, if any, the size of the swing has on the time of the swing. If you think that the size of the swing makes no difference you are in for a surprise, for there actually is a difference. It can amount to as much as 10% between small and wide swings.

If you would like to make a pendulum with a period of 4 seconds the thread must be 2^2 (i.e. 4 times) as long as the thread with a period of 2 seconds.

8. It happens on the dot

You will need: heavy book, 2 pieces of string.

Hang up a book, a cushion or a heavy parcel by two strings as is shown in the picture. Do you think it is possible to set the heavy thing swinging without touching it in any way? Swinging really well, not just a feeble movement from side to side?

It looks impossible doesn't it? But it can be done, provided that you use not your intelligence this time . . . but your breath! You can get this heavy thing swinging strongly by . . . blowing on it!

You don't believe it? But it's true! And you don't

need to blow hard. What really matters is that you blow at precisely the right moment.

Shall we begin? Blow once against the book or whatever it is that you have hung up. This will make it swing a very small distance. Have you ever noticed just how a swinging object actually behaves? It is moving at its fastest in the middle of its swing, and gradually slows down until it reaches the top of its swing when, for a fraction of a second, it actually comes to rest. Then it starts to move back again with increasing speed in the opposite direction.

Now if you blow immediately after the object stops, and continue to do it at exactly the same instant several times, even with the insignificant force of your breath you can get the heavy object swinging as hard as you like. Anybody who is good at swinging himself will be aware of this fact already. In this example the force itself is not very important – the 'critical moment', that's the secret. A swinging book like this, or any swinging object, has its own particular time of swing, or period, which is dependent on the length of string or whatever is supporting it. If the number of little pushes per minute is the same as the number of swings per minute then the size of the swings can be enormous.

This phenomenon is known as resonance and occurs in many different ways. For example, because of its elasticity and its few supports a bridge has a regular period of vibration. Some people think that soldiers should not march in step when crossing a bridge because the rate of steps might be the same as the resonant frequency of the bridge. In this case the bridge must start to swing violently and eventually collapse. In fact the likelihood of this happening is rather remote because the resonant frequency of a bridge is far lower than that of a marching pace. But this effect is much more likely with less sturdy objects. A patient on a stretcher might jog uncomfortably when the two stretcher-bearers walk in step; and I must confess that I myself once made a small, strong, steel suspension bridge in Ceylon resonate so strongly by walking across it at a certain pace that the deck of the bridge moved dangerously for a few moments and I was afraid that the bridge – and I with it! – would be thrown into the ravine.

As we shall see later, resonance plays a very large part in music and other sounds. The wonder of radio and its tuning depend to an important degree on resonance.

9. The immovable tower

You will need: draughts, ruler or thin flat object.

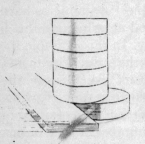

Perhaps this rather spectacular demonstration was discovered by some mischievous boy who tried to knock down, with a blow from a ruler, the tower of draughts which his little brother had just built. Did he find that when he struck at what seemed to be the most vulnerable part, the bottom, just one draught flew out and the rest of the tower stayed upright? If it did happen that way I am pretty sure that the boy's fit of temper was gone in a flash at such a surprising experience.

On a table without a cloth set up a pile of about eight draughts. Now with a flat ruler, or some other thin flat object, strike a smart blow at the bottom draught. You will knock the draught away and the pile will drop down the thickness of one draught without falling over. You have to strike your blow in just the right way, however, and that may need a little practice.

Of course you must only touch the bottom draught with the *side* of the ruler, so use one that is less than

16

half the thickness of a draught. It is safest to swing the ruler horizontally just a fraction above the surface of the table, and then you can be sure that you will hit the bottom draught fairly and squarely.

Now that you have knocked the bottom draught away without the tower falling over, what next? Try again, hitting the draught which is now at the bottom. You will be able to go on doing this several times.

How is all this possible? It is obvious why you can knock one light draught away, but the reason the remainder of the pile remains upright is because of inertia – the unwillingness of all objects to be moved from their places. This unwillingness, or inertia, increases with the weight (or more correctly, the 'mass') of the object.

10. Which will you break? The hairs or the stick?

You will need: 2 long hairs or very thin threads, thin wooden stick, 2 chairs, heavy metal or wooden object with thin edge.

Ask one of the ladies of your household for a couple of long strands of hair – she won't miss them! – and use them to hang a thin wooden stick from two chairs. (If you cannot get long enough hairs use very thin thread.) Tie a hair round each end of the stick, making sure the knots are fast, and tie each of the other ends of hair to a chair.

What will happen if you give a sharp blow to the

centre of the stick with a heavy piece of wood, or some heavy metal object, with a thin edge? If you expect the hairs or threads to break, you will be wrong. For, to your great surprise, the hairs hold out best and if you hit hard enough the piece of wood breaks!

Are the hairs stronger than the wood then? Not at all. Once again it is inertia which provides the explanation. Remember inertia?–a body's resistance to motion. The stick is so reluctant to move that it breaks rather than move downwards.

11. Where does the coin fall?

You will need: a glass, playing card, postcard or piece of smooth card, coin.

Place a playing card on top of a glass and then lay a coin on it. What will happen if you flick the card away smartly with your finger? What will happen to the coin? Where will it fall?

Probably you will say that the coin sticks with the card as it flies off and they then tumble separately on to the table. The card certainly does fall, but as for the coin. . . . Well, try it and see.

If you flick the card away fast enough the coin drops right into the glass. It does not go with the card but

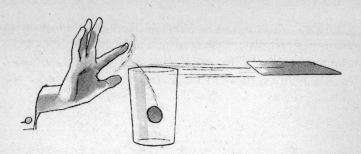

stays behind, following the principle of inertia. And once the card has gone the coin obeys the law of gravity and falls into the glass.

12. The wandering coin

You will need: thin coin (1p), 2 thicker coins (2p's), a glass, table with tablecloth.

On a table covered with a tablecloth lay a 1p piece and two 2p pieces. Place a glass over them as is shown in the drawing. Is it possible now to get the 1p from under the glass without touching either the glass or the two 2p pieces.

'Ah,' says some Smart Aleck, 'Blow!' But blow as hard as you like – you'll never do it. A magnet? Just try. Nothing happens. Despite all your efforts the 1p piece refuses to budge. Well then, how are we going to get it out?

Of course you could bore a large hole from underneath the table but I imagine the family would not be too pleased about that! It would mean an awful lot of work, too. However, it would be quite unnecessary because there is a delightfully simple way of getting the 1p out from under the glass. You just make it walk out. . . .

Because the 2p's on which the glass is resting are thicker than the 1p there is enough room beneath the edge of the glass to let the 1p through. How are we going to make it walk? By scraping the cloth with your fingernails towards you, close to the side of the glass. You see! The 1p comes walking towards you, and it is not long before it is right out from under the glass.

How does it work? With each scrape of your finger you drag the tablecloth forward a little, bringing the 1p with it. But when you lift your finger, the elasticity of the cloth makes it spring back while the 1p, thanks to its inertia, stays where it is – on the spot it was drawn to by the cloth. So, each time you scrape, the 1p comes a little nearer, until in the end it is right out.

13. A flywheel from a button

You will need: very large button, very strong thread or thin string.

Because of the phenomenon of inertia an object which is in motion is not easy to stop – it tends to continue as it is. Advantage is taken of this in engineering whenever a flywheel is used. A flywheel is a very heavy metal wheel. Once it is whirling round at high speed, very little power is required to keep it moving. It plays a very important part in, for instance, a steam engine.

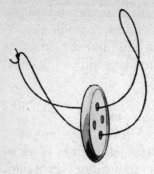

We are going to make a small flywheel. Insert about a yard of strong thread or thin string through opposite holes of a large button, and knot the ends together. Now take hold of the thread either side of the button (which should be in the centre) between thumb and forefinger of each hand. Swing the button round several times in the same direction so that the double threads twist round one another.

If you now pull hard on the threads the button spins round very fast and if you hold your hands still you will notice that when the threads are untwisted once more the button, because of its flywheel action, continues to spin and so winds up the threads again in the opposite direction. Now, if you pull your hands again at exactly the right moment, the button spins faster still. You can keep this going for as long as you like provided that you pull your hands apart at precisely the right moment. The button spins so fast that you hear a buzzing or sizzling sound and you get the feeling that the thread has become as elastic as rubber.

Try this experiment with buttons of different sizes or with a circle of plywood in which you have cut a

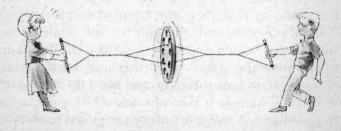

couple of little holes. In order to be able to pull better you could put a couple of short sticks at the ends of the thread to form handles. The speed of rotation can be enormous, and you can make a noise like a miniature whirlwind or a high-pitched note like a humming-top.

14. Your jet engine runs on . . . water

You will need: tin without a lid, nail, button with three holes, thin string, tap.

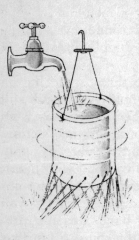

The powerful jet engines of aeroplanes run on paraffin (kerosene). When it burns it releases a stream of hot gases which rush in a backwards direction with great power and speed. In accordance with Newton's Third Law of Motion, which states that every action has an equal and opposite reaction, the backward motion of the escaping gases produces a forward motion of the aeroplane.

You can demonstrate the principle of jet propulsion very neatly with a tin in which you have punched a series of evenly spaced holes just above the bottom rim. When you have punched each hole give the nail a wrench as far as possible to the left so that the opening makes an angle with the side of the tin.

At the upper edge of the tin make a couple of holes and pass a thin string through each. Knot the ends of the string so that they don't pull through the holes. Thread the other ends through the outer holes of your three-holed button and knot them as well. Push a nail up through the centre hole (the head must be large enough not to pass through) and bend the nail over so that it will hang in a loop of string which you can hold in your hand. Now your water jet engine is ready.

Hang the tin under the tap. Turn on the tap and when the tin is full adjust the tap so that the water does not overflow but squirts out steadily at the bottom. As your holes are at an angle the water squirts out sideways, and because of the force of reaction the tin spins round in the opposite direction – jet propulsion, just like modern aeroplanes. You see the same principle at work in many lawn-sprinklers.

15. Acrobatic forks

You will need: glass, long nail, 2 forks, cork, bottle with cap.

It is good fun to make all sorts of things balance on points or narrow edges. Usually it can be done by supporting the object, or hanging it, at its Centre of Gravity. The Centre of Gravity is an imaginary point through which the whole weight of an object seems to act. In a straight stick of even thickness – like a ruler – the Centre of Gravity is exactly in the middle. You can find the Centre of Gravity of other long objects, such as an umbrella, a spoon, or a fork, by balancing them on your finger so that they remain horizontal. When the Centre of Gravity and the point of support are together the body remains in equilibrium, i.e. balanced.

Does this hold for the following demonstration? We shall see. Stick two forks and a nail into a cork as is shown in the drawing, and place the nail on the rim of a glass, adjusting its position until the whole lot remains in equilibrium. No matter how impossible it may look it works because the Centre of Gravity of the

whole arrangement of cork, forks and nail lies at or just below the point of support.

You can also get the forks, stuck in the cork, to balance vertically as the second drawing shows. You can do it on the top of a bottle with a cap. If you make a small dent in the cap, and use a nail with a round head, or a needle, you can make the whole contraption spin round. And here too the Centre of Gravity is at or below the point of support.

16. What a complicated equilibrium!

You will need: 2 knives, 2 pencils, 2 penholders with nibs, thread.

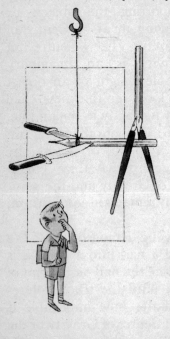

For fans of balancing experiments here is a really fascinating one. First push the points of two knives into a pencil with a long sharp point. The knives must make the same angle with the pencil and be exactly opposite each other.

Do the same thing with the two penholders and another pencil with a long sharp point. You will see the idea in the drawing. The nibs should be stuck into the pencil close to the point. Hang the first arrangement in the loop of a slack thread. Hold the right-hand end of

24

the pencil to steady it and put the second pencil point on it. It may be necessary to make a small hole at the end of the first pencil in order to make sure that the second pencil stays in position.

When it is all hanging nicely on the thread you will view it with a great deal of pleasure and satisfaction. Isn't this an attractive way of storing your knives, pencils and pens? You have no need to search. . . .

17. The marvel of centrifugal force

You will need: circular washing-up bowl, circular metal dish with sloping sides, washing-up mop, water, milk.

When you have helped with the washing-up one evening you can do a very interesting experiment. You will need the washing-up bowl. It should be perfectly round and have vertical sides. One of the soft plastic bowls is best for our purpose. Now pour a cupful of milk into a metal dish with sloping sides which should be a little smaller than the bowl. Next pour enough water into the bowl for the dish to float in it without its touching the side of the bowl. The object is that the dish should be able to spin round easily – very fast!

But how are we to get the dish to spin? By pressing on the sloping side of the dish with the washing-up mop and giving a circular motion. With a bit of practice you will find that you can make the dish spin round at a terrific speed and that when you stop your movement it continues to spin for quite a long time on its 'floating bearing'. But even more remarkable. . . .

When you began to spin the dish you saw a layer of milk on the bottom about half an inch deep. But once the dish started to spin round the bottom was bone-dry! Not a drop of milk was to be seen there – it had all whirled out to cover the sloping side of the dish: a surprising sight! This continues until the dish is spinning so slowly that the milk is no longer thrown outwards by the centrifugal force and so flows back towards the middle.

Yes, it is the centrifugal force which we have to thank for this experiment. The force which we feel when we swing some heavy object round on the end of a string. It is just as if it were being pulled outwards – the centrifugal force. This same force which makes it possible to swing a bucket of water round in a vertical circle without the water falling out even when the open top of the bucket is underneath. The water is pressed against the bottom of the bucket by the centrifugal force.

One of the most delightful applications of centrifugal force is to be seen at a fairground in the gigantic cylinder, rotating round a vertical axis, with a bottom which can be lowered. You stand against the side of the cylinder, the cylinder begins to spin round, the floor is lowered from beneath you, and you stick to the wall like a fly. If you take something out of your pocket and try to drop it, it too is pressed against the wall by the centrifugal force. This force finds great application in industry for the separation of liquids and the heavier particles in them, for instance milk and cream. The heavier parts are flung outwards farther than the lighter.

18. Ounce, lift up a pound

You will need: loop of thread, strong thin string, 2 weights, one light and one heavy, cotton reel.

Can an ounce lift up a pound? Certainly, and more, with the help of centrifugal force.

For this experiment we shall need a light and a heavy object – one should be about ten times as heavy as the other. For your light weight you can use anything small that can be whirled round without danger. This does not apply to the heavy object for it is only going to be lifted up. You could use a book, a brick or something of metal.

Push a piece of strong thin string (the white sisal string used for parcels has proved highly satisfactory) about 30 inches long through the hole in a cotton reel and tie the two objects to the ends. Take hold of the reel in such a way that your hand also grips the string underneath. Let the heavy weight hang about a foot below the reel. Then start to rotate the hand holding the reel in a horizontal circle above your head so that the small weight goes round too – like a whirling lasso. The faster it goes the better, for then the centrifugal force is greater.

When the small weight is swinging round fast you will find you need no longer grip the string below the reel. Then you will see the heavy weight being lifted up – the fast moving small weight lifting up the heavy one – an ounce lifting a pound! But make sure the string is strong enough, for if it breaks. . . .

You remember the story of little David who had a fight to the death with the giant Goliath. Just as an ounce can overcome a pound so the little David overcame Goliath, thanks to the same centrifugal force. With a sling, both ends held in his hand, David swung a stone round so fast that when he let it go it struck the giant's forehead with such a force that he fell down dead. . . .

19. John speaking to Margaret is a rather complicated affair.

John says a few words, Margaret listens – there's nothing to it! And yet, if we think about what has actually taken place, these apparently simple actions turn out to be amazingly complicated.

It all begins in John's brain, which thinks up the message John wants to give Margaret. Thousands of brain cells work at it and then send a mass of different orders along the nerves to the organs in John's body (his lungs, his vocal cords and his mouth), which will turn his message for Margaret into sound.

If a gale blows through electric wires or branches of trees, we hear a whistling sound. There's even a musical instrument, the Aeolian harp, that works like this. It consists of strings through which the wind is allowed to blow, producing musical sounds.

Now, there's an Aeolian harp in John's larynx, as there is in yours and everybody else's as well. This human Aeolian harp consists of two small pieces of elastic muscle which are called the vocal cords. But their 'wind' comes from the lungs, which blow air continually through the vocal cords, like life-long bellows, which never stop working. Normally the vocal cords are so slack, and so far apart, that when we breath out, the air can go through them without there being any sound.

But being muscles the vocal cords can be brought closer together and stretched more tightly. The stream of air then pushes the vocal cords a little apart, but through their elasticity they spring back, are again pushed apart, spring back again, and this repeats itself so quickly that the vocal cords vibrate. The air, therefore, which goes through them also vibrates and air vibrations are formed – sound waves.

What is sound?

All sounds, without exception, are created because something is vibrating. Whether it's the chirruping of the birds, the roar of a car or aeroplane, the buzzing of bees, the rumbling of thunder, the barking of dogs, the talking, laughing, shouting or singing of humans, the squeaking of a door or the music from a wireless or musical instruments – all these sounds come into existence because air is made to vibrate by the source of the sound.

However, to get back to John; after the message for Margaret has been worked out by his brain, it sends orders along the nerves to the little muscles of the vocal cords, telling them how tightly or loosely stretched and how close together they must be. The tighter the vocal cords are stretched by these muscles, the faster they vibrate and the higher the sound becomes. Vocal cords which are less tightly stretched vibrate more slowly and give lower sounds.

The faster something vibrates, the higher the sound it produces. That's why the buzzing of a mosquito

with its small, quickly moving wings sounds much higher than the droning of the more slowly moving bee. If something vibrates tens of times per second, then we hear a low tone. If it vibrates many hundreds or thousands of times per second, a high tone rings out. We can hear sounds from about 20 to about 20,000 vibrations per second. Middle 'C' on a piano has 256 vibrations per second.

Back to John once more. His brain has sent a whole lot of orders via the nerves, not only to his vocal cords, but also to his tongue, lips, cheeks and jaws: in other words, to the hollows of his mouth and jaws and to his nasal and forehead cavities! What kind of orders! Orders as to how they must move and the shape they must give to these hollows. For these hollows act as sound-boxes which amplify the sounds coming from the vocal cords and give them a distinct timbre – sound colour. You must have noticed how sometimes a bath-room, a cellar or a church makes sounds louder or more resonant.

You can find out how important the shape and the movements of the mouth are if you try to talk without moving your mouth. Everything that you say sounds quite different and certain sounds, most of the consonants especially, can't be pronounced at all. Another interesting experiment is to press a couple of fingers against your larynx – your Adam's apple – and make high and low, as well as soft and loud noises. Then you will clearly feel the vibrations, quick ones for the high tones, slower for the low tones, weak vibrations for a soft sound and strong ones when you shout.

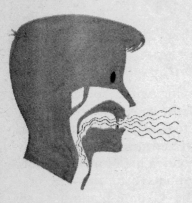

John's brain takes all this into account. It has told the lungs how hard they must blow the air through the vocal cords, it has ordered the muscles of the vocal cords to make the latter vibrate fairly strongly – not too much because Margaret might be startled, not too little because then she wouldn't hear anything. John, however, isn't the sort of boy that whispers, but he does like to put cordiality into his voice – especially when he says something to Margaret. The muscles of his mouth and nasal cavities can be trusted to take care of this!

But we must keep to the point. Sound waves, then come out of John's mouth – John is speaking. John's voice is heard coming from that mouth. We've seen how the speech is produced that Margaret hears. . . .

At the receiving end

Wait a minute though – we're going just a bit too quickly! For a great deal has to happen before Margaret hears and knows what John is saying. The sound waves coming out of John's mouth spread in all directions and also reach Margaret's ears. What happens then?

You can't see the sound waves, because these waves are made in air, which happens to be invisible. But they are very like waves on water, and they move in much the same way. Just throw a stone into a pond and you'll see how circular waves form and spread out concentrically. Waves of water move at about just over 3 feet per second. Sound waves on the other hand move much more quickly – at about 1,100 feet per second!

If you dip the tip of your index finger very quickly in and out of a bowl of water, little circular waves of water will spread out, and in just the same way John's vibrating vocal cords make sound waves spread out in the air. If these waves of water reach a piece of floating wood or paper, then it rocks. The sound waves coming out of John's mouth also make something rock, or vibrate: Margaret's eardrums! At the same time they're concentrated by Margaret's shell-shaped external ears – or auricles – and the trumpet-shaped passage leading into her ears – the acoustic canal.

Waves of water are really made up of particles of water which go alternately up and down and in the same way sound waves are made up of air which quickly and alternately condenses and thins. The higher pressure of the condensed air pushes the eardrum in. When the air thins again the drum is pushed out by the air on the other side of the drum in the middle ear. As this alternates very quickly, the sound waves make the eardrum vibrate.

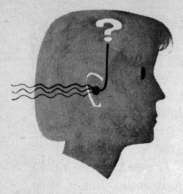

What Margaret calls her 'ear' is only the auricle and the acoustic canal, and these do nothing more than receive all sound waves. Her proper ear, her real hearing organ, is inside Margaret's skull. It begins with the eardrum, which converts the sound waves into mechanical vibrations. These vibrations are conveyed by three levers – the tympanic bones, called the hammer, anvil and stirrup – to a second drum, which is the 'oval window' of a rolled-up pipe looking like a snail shell and filled with fluid. The vibrating of the oval window makes waves in the fluid and these move the tympanic cords or 'Organ of Corti', which, small as it is, is one of the greatest of Nature's wonders.

The harp of 24,000 strings

That Organ of Corti in Margaret's ear, and in everybody else's ear as well, is like a miniature harp or miniature grand piano, with no less than . . . 24,000 strings! Believe it or not, there are about 24,000 gossamer strings stretched over a length of only $\frac{3}{5}$ inch and they are only a few hundredths of an inch in length. And each of them, just as with a real harp or piano, is tuned to a different pitch. And not only that, each of those 24,000 strings is connected to Margaret's brain by

34

means of a separate nerve. In that Organ of Corti and in the brain, that is where the wonder of hearing takes place.

Margaret's external ears pick up, besides John's voice, many other sounds: music from the wireless, the singing of birds and the roar of passing cars. The Organ of Corti sorts out the various sound vibrations from this medley and passes on to Margaret's brain the sounds which have been picked up. How does this work?

The medley of sound waves makes the eardrum vibrate. These extremely intricate vibrations make equally intricate waves in the fluid of the snail shell, via the tympanic bones and the oval window, and move along the 24,000 strings of the Organ of Corti. Not all of the strings vibrate through this. Only certain cords. Which are those?

Let's take it that amongst the sounds which John produces while talking, there is one with 256 vibrations per second – that is to say at the pitch of the musical note 'middle C'. That sound is made because John's vocal cords vibrated to and fro 256 times per second. This produced sound waves with air condensing and thinning 256 times per second, making Margaret's eardrum vibrate 256 times per second. This stirred up 256 waves per second in the fluid in the snail shell and now, of all those 24,000 strings, only the cord which is tuned to 256 vibrations per second vibrates. Although those waves also pass along the other cords, these stay still. You can imitate this phenomenon yourself.

Go and sit down at a piano. Press your foot down on the right pedal so that all the strings are open. Then sing very loudly one short note. Afterwards listen carefully and you'll hear that same note coming from the piano. If you sing another short note loudly, you'll notice this second note resounding in the piano. You can do the same experiment with a guitar, but then you must choose the pitch of one of the six guitar strings. Sing at the pitch of the third string for example and you'll notice that only that string resounds; the other strings are silent. Yes, you can even feel that one string vibrating, while others are still.

Exactly the same happens with that miniature piano, the Organ of Corti. Each of its 24,000 strings is tuned to a different pitch and if John's vocal cords vibrate successively 435, 216 and 322 times a second, then the strings tuned to 435, 216 and 322 vibrations per second will vibrate. Each of these cords then sends the message 'I'm vibrating' through the nerve attached to Margaret's brain. In this way Margaret is conscious of the fact that she's hearing these three notes!

So this is how it works. Each of those 24,000 strings is attached to Margaret's brain by means of a separate nerve so that they can inform the brain exactly as to the nature and the composition of the sound which has reached her eardrum. Because her brain has been so well informed, Margaret knows what John has said to her.

Two more questions . . .

Now, having settled *that* there are still two important questions to be answered.

The first is this: why has Margaret got *two* ears? Is this little lady so demanding that she doesn't consider one ear to be enough? After all, she can hear everything with one ear! It must be said for Margaret that she isn't the only person with two ears. There are others. All the same, the question of that second ear does need explaining.

Margaret's second ear isn't a reserve ear which can be used if she should lose the first one. It doesn't help her to hear more clearly. Then what is it for? Her second ear has been most useful to Margaret. For instance, there was that time when she went so far into the forest while John sat at the roadside reading, that she got lost. She called out in fright and because John called back, she knew where he was sitting and knew exactly in which direction she had to go. But how did she know that?

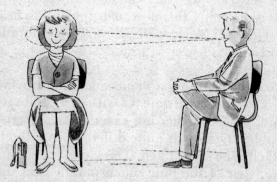

Thanks to that second ear! Her one ear couldn't have told her. For that matter her second ear couldn't either. But her two ears *together* could – they told Margaret's brain where the source of the sound, John, was! It's the same in the sitting-room. Even if Margaret closes her eyes and John wanders around while he's speaking, she can determine exactly where he is. How?

Imagine that John is sitting to the left of her. Margaret's left ear is then about 8 inches nearer John's mouth than her right ear and the sound waves from John's voice reach her left ear a little sooner than her right ear – about 1/1500 of a second sooner – and at the same time her left ear hears the sound a little louder than her right ear. These minute differences in volume and time between what the right and the left ears hear, are what make Margaret and everyone else aware of the direction from which the sound comes. Because we can hear stereophonically with our two ears and because we know by experience how loud a sound is when it comes from a certain distance, we are able to locate the source of the sound – to determine its position pretty accurately!

The second question. Nearly all sounds which are of importance to Margaret and to us all in our daily lives, have between 30 and 5,000 vibrations per second. What is the point, therefore, of being able to hear much higher notes? Notes with up to 20,000 vibrations per second? The answer is, in order to hear the so-called overtones!

Take for example a violin and a flute which both produce the musical note 'C' with its 256 vibrations per second. Their pitches are exactly the same. And yet the violin 'C' sounds quite different from the flute 'C' of exactly the same pitch. The violin 'C' sounds much richer, that of the flute much purer. That difference is caused by the overtones (or harmonics). They determine the quality, the colour of the sound – the timbre.

The violin string vibrating to and fro 256 times per second makes sound waves with a multiple of that number of vibrations, i.e. 512, 768, 1,024, 1,280, etc.

vibrations per second. These are the overtones and the original note with the 256 vibrations is called the fundamental note. A flute also has overtones, but these are less loud than those of a violin and that's why a flute has a purer note. Different instruments have overtones of different strengths and relative proportions of strength and from this each instrument derives its own, characteristic sound. The human voice also produces overtones but this also varies from person to person according to the strength and relative proportion of strength. That's why even blindfold we can recognize people by the sound of their voices.

. . . and an answer

Margaret can pick John's voice out of a thousand others. She doesn't think about it particularly, any more than she does about the complicated wonder of speaking and hearing. She's never gone into all that because she takes speaking and hearing for granted. How it is 'granted' will be more or less clear to you now that we've followed in five pages the story of how John says something and Margaret takes it in. The only thing we don't know yet is what John said to her. At long last it can be revealed!

'Would you like some lemonade?'

What was Margaret's answer? She doesn't know much about natural science. She couldn't care less about it, in fact. How vocal cords vibrate, what causes sound waves, what the Organ of Corti does and what overtones are – she's just not interested. All the same, she's a girl with plenty of understanding, and because she knows that eleven pages have been written just about John's question, 'Would you like some lemon-ade?' and she intends to avoid the repetition of such a detailed explanation, she answers with a nod. A nod of acceptance.

20. Make your own xylophone

You will need: wood, 2 strips of foam rubber, tools.

There are very few instruments which you can make as easily as a xylophone. It consists of bars of wood of different lengths resting on springy supports. If you tap the bars of wood with a small hammer, the elasticity of the wood makes it vibrate and give out very pleasant sounds. The pitch of the note depends upon the length of the wooden bar, the shorter it is, the higher the note.

The cheapest deal will do quite well. Oak, beech or birch are not suitable. Parana pine, mahogany, and rosewood give the most beautiful notes. But ordinary deal is very good; or you can use lime or poplar.

You start with some bars of wood, about $\frac{3}{4}$ inch thick and about $1\frac{1}{2}$ inches wide. They must be made as smooth as possible with glass paper, and all the corners and sharp edges must be slightly rounded. How big shall we make the xylophone? With eight bars so that you can play an octave, e.g. C-D-E-F-G-A-B-C? With twelve bars for C-D-E-F-G-A-B-C-D-E-F-G? Or two octaves? Or perhaps you would like to make a more complete xylophone with twenty-five so that you can play sharps and flats as well? For instance: G-G♯-A-B♭-B-C-C♯-D-E♭-E-F-F♯-G-G♯-A-B♭-B-C-C♯-D-E♭-E-F-F♯-G, which are the same as the black and white notes of the piano. You will be able to play quite a lot of different tunes then.

The number of bars will determine the length of the strips of foam rubber or plastic that you will need for supports. Cut pieces out of the foam rubber so that the wooden bars will fit nicely into them. Now for the bars themselves. So that you can cut them to exactly the right lengths you will need not only a saw but a musical instrument such as a piano or an accordion; at a pinch a well-tuned guitar or violin will do, or even a flute. With a bar between 12 and 14 inches long, according to the kind of wood, you can get a note corresponding to middle C on the piano. If you decide to have middle C as the lowest note of your xylophone cut a piece of wood about $14\frac{1}{2}$ inches long, lay it across the rubber strips and strike it with a small hammer. Compare the pitch of the note which it makes with the middle C of the piano or the C of another instrument.

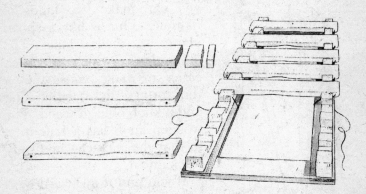

It will be a real stroke of luck if the notes are exactly the same. More likely the note from the wood will be too low. Saw a little bit off the end. How's that? Or is the note still too low? Saw another bit off and continue doing this until you get exactly the right note. Hollow out the middle of the wood a little with a rasp, a file or a knife and sandpaper as is shown in the drawing. This improves the tone. However, you must take into account the fact that the note is made lower by this hollowing out. By hollowing, cutting off, smoothing the sides with sandpaper and rounding the edges slightly you can get your piece of wood exactly in tune with the C of the instrument. You can get a high degree of accuracy by filing only a small amount off your strip of wood. And do not worry in the least if, in spite of working very carefully, the tone of the wood turns out to be too high. You can easily lower it again by hollowing it out a little more.

In this manner you can work bar by bar until all together they give a beautiful, pure musical scale. The bars must be supported at about $\frac{2}{9}$ of their lengths from each end by the rubber. This means that the strips of rubber must be closer together under the higher notes.

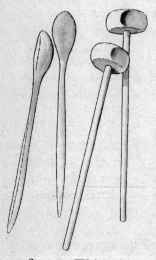

For playing your xylophone you can make two kinds of hammer. One is like a spoon about 10 inches long. The other kind, which is much easier to make, consists of a thin springy stick 9 inches long and a knob of hard wood. The wooden knob has a hole in it so that the stick can be firmly stuck into it.

If you find it awkward having everything in the xylophone loose, the strips of foam rubber can be stuck to a wooden frame. This will make it easier to move the instrument about. It is possible, too, to secure the wooden bars a little more firmly. You can do this as shown in the drawing, by boring a hole in each end of each bar, threading a short string through and then winding the string round the rubber and the frame. Should you decide to make a large xylophone so that you can play the sharps and flats, you can darken the semitones (those which correspond to the black notes on the piano) with some stain so that you will be able to distinguish them easily. It is quite a good idea to write the name of each note on the wood with a ball pen.

When you have acquired sufficient skill at playing with one hand you can try with two so that you can play harmonies. Hold the hammers firmly between thumb and first finger.

The way to amplify the notes of your xylophone by resonance is explained in *Thanks to resonance* (page 50).

21. How to make a Swanee whistle

You will need: piece of plastic tube, piece of wooden curtain rod, cycle spoke, piece of rubber, leather or felt, piece of tin, screw, gummed paper or tape, tools.

While in the ordinary flute or recorder the pitch of the notes is altered by closing or opening one or more holes, in the Swanee whistle it is done by moving a piston in or out. The further it is moved out, the lower the note. Try to get a piece of plastic conduit tubing from an electrician or a piece of plastic water piping from a plumber. The tube should be about $9\frac{1}{2}$ inches long. Then you will need a piece of wooden curtain rod or dowel, just over 2 inches long, which is a nice close fit inside the tube, but will still slide up and down. Cut off a piece 1 inch long and bore a hole in the middle of each end. From a piece of tin cut a disc slightly smaller than the rod, and from a piece of rubber, leather or felt cut a disc with a diameter slightly greater than that of the rod. Now fix the two discs with a screw through their centres to one end of the 1-inch rod. The rubber disc goes next to the wood with the tin disc on the outside. Push the point of the spoke into the other end and tap it with a hammer to make sure it is firmly fixed. Now the piston is ready.

Saw off one end of the plastic tube at a slant (this is the mouthpiece), and $\frac{5}{8}$ inch from the same end make a very careful cut at right angles to the tube. Then very carefully cut down towards it at a slant – see the drawing. Cut a piece off the rest of the round rod and file one side of it flat by about $\frac{1}{16}$ inch. Now push it into the mouthpiece. If it is too loose, you can pack it with a little cellulose tape stuck to the round part. Push it into the tube so that the end comes in line with the vertical cut. Then cut or saw off any wood which still sticks out of the end of the tube. Cut it off at an angle. Look at the drawing again.

Now if you blow through the mouthpiece while you close the other end of the tube with your finger you should hear a whistling note. The next thing is to replace your finger by the piston. Push the piston into the tube; the spoke will act as a piston rod. Blow again and as you move the piston in and out you will get different notes.

Everything all right? Then we can complete our whistle by slipping over the end of the spoke a piece of the round rod with a hole bored in it. The rod can have a bit of gummed paper or tape stuck round it so that it will stay firmly in the plastic tube; it will then prevent the piston falling right out. Of course the hole must be large enough to allow the spoke to slide through it easily. Then bend the spoke, and make a loop in the end to fit your thumb. Now for some diligent practising, merry tunes, tremolos and birdcalls. The range of the whistle is two octaves.

22. A string bass from a box and a piece of string

You will need: box, some pieces of wood, piece of strong string, screws and tools.

Whistle solo with xylophone accompaniment . . . we need a bass as well! Then we shall have a trio and, what's more, with lovely deep notes that you can feel in the pit of your stomach.

In view of the fact that a real double-bass like the musicians use is rather dear, we will make our own from a box. Excellent for this purpose is a tea-chest, one of those large cubical boxes made of plywood in which tea is packed. You may be able to get one from a tea-merchant, a removal firm, or even from school. They are often used for the delivery of stationery. If you can't get a tea-chest, try to obtain some other large box with thin sides. Make sure that the box is firmly constructed so that none of it rattles. If it does, you will have to get to work with a few screws or glue to get rid of the rattle. We will not need the lid for the time being, so take it off. The bottom of the box is going to be the top of our bass.

Next you will need a strong, well planed piece of wood about 1 inch thick, 2 inches wide and about $5\frac{1}{2}$ feet long. You can use deal, but a harder wood such as parana pine is better. Take off the sharp edges with a piece of glass paper wrapped round a block of wood, and rub the wood until it has a really smooth surface. In the upper end of the wood make a notch with a saw, a file or even a knife, and about 3 inches from the top screw a wooden block to the wood.

Great care must be taken when you come to securing the long piece of wood to the tea-chest. The part of the box where the long piece is to be fixed must be reinforced with a strip of multi-ply wood about $\frac{1}{4}$ inch thick. Drill five equally spaced holes in this piece and countersink the holes to take woodscrews. Place this piece inside the box precisely where you want it to go. Mark the positions of the holes with a sharp pencil. Bore holes in the side of the box. Lay the long piece of wood on the ground, and place the box on top of it in exactly the right position. Inside the box put the strip of multi-ply wood. Now you can fasten the long piece and the reinforcement all together with woodscrews. You can make the joint even stronger by putting some glue on before you screw up. The place where the string is to be secured to the upper side of the box must also be reinforced from inside with a strip of plywood. When you have put the reinforcing piece in place, bore a hole through it and what is now the top of the box about $\frac{3}{8}$ inch in diameter, and file a groove from the hole in the direction of the upright piece of about $\frac{1}{8}$ inch wide. Now fasten the lid of the box on to the open underside of it.

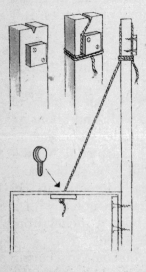

For your string you can use a piece of strong string, or nylon cord if you can get it, about $\frac{1}{8}$ inch thick. At one end of the string make a good strong knot. Push the knot through the round hole to the inside. The string will catch in the groove. Secure the other end of the string through the notch and round the block at the top of the upright. Do not stretch the string too tightly, for that will give too high a note which will not allow you to play the instrument well. By pressing on the string with the fingers of your left hand on a longer or shorter length you can produce low and high notes. It is quite easy to play a tune. A tea-chest bass has rather the character of a percussion instrument. As a rhythm instrument it is rather attractive.

23. Listen to the beat of your heart

You will need: funnel, piece of rubber tubing.

Have you heard of a machine which can work without stopping for more than seventy years? That is, without ever stopping at all? Your own heart is such a machine, a pump, driven by strong muscles. It beats more than 100,000 times every 24 hours, pumping some 3,000 gallons through your body! That is well over a million gallons in a year, and tens of millions in a lifetime. And although the heart is no bigger than a clenched fist it does as much work in a day as a man does in climbing to the top of a hundred-storey skyscraper. In the lifetime of a man that little heart produces enough energy to drive a great motor truck several times round the world.

If you place your hand on your chest you can feel the beat of your heart. But your heart makes noises too. It sounds just like 'lub-dup . . . lub-dup . . . lub-dup. . . .' The sound is caused by the closing of the valves, which behave rather like shutters. But how can you hear the sounds of your heart?

The answer is – by making something like the instrument which the doctor uses when he wants to listen to the noises in your chest: a stethoscope. To make it you use a funnel (perhaps you have one in the kitchen) and a short length of rubber tubing, not more than a yard long. Push one end of the tubing over the small end of the funnel, and hold the other end of the tubing in your ear. Place the funnel on your own chest or a friend's. You will be able to hear the voice of the heart: 'lub-dup . . . lub-dup . . . lub-dup. . . .'

The funnel and the tubing amplify the sound. You will notice this if you hold the funnel over a watch lying on the table. With your stethoscope you will be able to amplify dozens of other sounds, for instance, the sounds which insects make. Try to catch a fly or midge under your funnel!

24. And the bottle said 'Boo!'

You will need: some bottles, water.

That was the end of a fairy-tale, when the bottle said 'Boo!', but for us it is the beginning of a new experiment which will explain the action of the organ and other wind instruments. Blow across the neck of an empty bottle. If you do it in the right way, the bottle gives out a melodious 'Boo'; it makes a musical note.

How does it happen? Where the air, which you blow out, strikes the side of the bottle, small whirlwinds are set up like those you see in a stream of water when it runs against stones, setting up eddies and whirlpools. Where a stream of air meets a small obstruction these eddies in the air occur. It is them we have to thank for our organs, whistles, flutes and other wind instruments. Each of these miniature whirlwinds gives a push not only against the air, but also against the obstruction. Because of the rapid succession of these whirlwinds the air and the obstruction – in this case the side of the bottle – are set into vibration. Is this vibration, then, the sound that we hear? No.

These vibrations which occur have a wide range of different frequencies. (The frequency is the number of vibrations per second.) Yet only vibrations of *one particular* frequency will be audible; and the sound is caused because the whole volume of air in the bottle – or in the organ pipe, flute or other wind instrument – vibrates strongly. What that frequency is depends principally on the length of the column of air. The longer the column, the lower the note; the shorter the column, the higher the note.

You will observe this if you put some water in the bottle and blow across the top again. The note is higher than before because the air column is shorter now. By preparing a row of bottles, each containing a little more water than the previous one, you can make a whole musical scale. But what is the relationship between the length of the air column and the pitch (or frequency) of the note which is produced?

Very briefly, it is this: of the different sound vibrations which are set up at the mouth of the bottle, that note sounds loudest whose waves are reflected from the bottom of the bottle (or from the surface of the water) so as to reinforce the original wave, and set up what are known as *standing waves*. The drawing on the next page shows such a situation. If the length of the air column is one-quarter of a wavelength of a sound wave, such a strengthening of the sound results. The wavelength is always equal to the speed of sound, 1,100 feet per second, divided by the number of vibrations per second. The sound waves of a note with a frequency of 330 vibrations therefore have a wavelength of 3¼ feet, or 40 inches. So, if the air column is 10 inches long (i.e. a quarter of a wavelength), the end of a half-wave, which we call a node, coincides exactly with the point of reflection: the bottom of the bottle or the surface of the water in the bottle. The waves, moving towards that point, coincide with the reflected waves moving in the opposite direction, resulting in the formation of standing waves which sound very much louder than the original waves.

Standing waves like these are not only set up in columns of air closed at one end but also in columns open at both ends. This is what happens in open organ pipes and in most wind instruments. But the length of one of these pipes is not one-quarter, but a half, the wavelength of the note it produces.

An organ consists of many pipes of different lengths. The longer the pipe, the lower the note. In most wind instruments the length of the pipe can be altered in order to obtain the different notes. In a trombone this is done by sliding one of the tubes in or out of the other one; in a recorder by opening or closing holes in the pipe, and in clarinets, oboes, etc. by opening or closing holes with keys.

25. Thanks to resonance

You will need: 2 bottles, cardboard tubes.

If you press down the loud pedal of a piano and sing a note you can hear the same note coming from the piano. This is because one of the strings, tuned to that note, vibrates in sympathy with it. We call this phenomenon of sympathetic vibration *resonance*. This resonance occurs in many forms, and there is a scientific law which says: an object resonates when a note is sounded nearby of the same pitch as that which the object itself can produce.

The object can be a string, a column of air or an air-filled space. Take two similar bottles, for instance milk bottles. If you blow across the mouth of one bottle you hear a low note. This note, which sounds like 'Boo', you will remember from the previous experiment. If you hold your ear close to the other bottle, which is the same size, you will hear the same note sound – by resonance.

Think again about the experiment with the heavy book which you were able to set moving in large swings by carefully timed puffs of air. The same thing happens with a string or a column of air which resonates. Just as a pendulum of a certain length swings with a definite period so a string or air column has a definite period of vibration, for example 1/100 second. Such a string or air column vibrates most readily at 100 vibrations per second; so if another source of sound emits 100 waves per second these give tiny thrusts at just the right moments to make the string or air column vibrate strongly. Hence we get the standing waves which we spoke of in the previous experiment.

Resonance, then, is the strong vibration which arises when a very small force is applied again and again, at just the right instant, to an object which can be made to vibrate.

It is said that a singer with a powerful voice can cause a glass to shatter if he or she sings loudly a note which the glass itself can emit: resonance! Resonance is also the cause of the effect you sometimes get when the piano is being played; certain articles vibrate quite strongly and make noises.

Resonance is caused not only by sound waves, but by radio waves as well. In fact, when you tune a radio set to a certain station all you do is to bring the radio set into resonance with the transmitter – though in this case you are dealing with hundreds of thousands of vibrations a second.

You can increase the volume of the sound from your home-made xylophone by hanging beneath the wooden bars tubes of cardboard or plastic, or metal tubes of different lengths, the longest for the deeper notes. You will have to find by trial and error the length at which each tube resonates best. You can use either open tubes or tubes closed at the bottom; the former need to be half the length of closed tubes.

26. Make a model of sound waves

You will need: brass wire, broom handle, 2 wooden laths, thin thread, glass marbles, cellulose tape.

In the transmission of sound through the air the waves move at 1,100 feet per second. These sound waves consist of alternate compressions and rarefactions of the air. Consequently the particles of the air vibrate backwards and forwards but they do not travel with the sound. One particle strikes against the next and so the vibration progresses. By making a model we shall be able to understand it more easily.

Fasten threads to six glass marbles with cellulose tape and hang them up as shown in the drawing. Now pull the first marble to one side, and let go. It swings back and hits the second marble. This swings to one side, and then collides with the third one which gives the fourth one a little push. So it goes on, the motion being transferred by successive collisions.

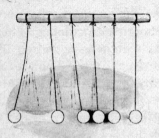

The same thing happens in the transmission of sound. A particle of air which is displaced by a vibrating vocal cord or string collides with the next one, which in turn strikes the next one; so, by the displacement of the air particles by one another, the sound vibrations are transmitted.

Your model also shows the compressions and rarefactions of the air. Two marbles, striking each other, represent a compression; two marbles swinging apart again represent a rarefaction. In the drawing the compressions are dark and the rarefactions white.

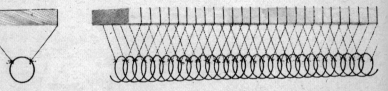

You can make a rather more intricate model from brass wire to demonstrate the motion of sound waves. Form a long helix, or spring, by winding brass wire round a broom handle or some similar thick stick.

Hang each turn of the helix by two threads from two horizontal laths. If you move one end of the helix horizontally backwards and forwards you will see a compression and a rarefaction travel along it. Each turn of wire represents a part of the air.

27. Reflection of sound

You will need: watch, 2 cardboard tubes, sheet of card, small board or book, radio, 2 umbrellas.

You know already that sound waves can be reflected by a wall, a cliff or a wood. An echo is, of course, just such a sound reflection.

As in the case of light waves, the angle of reflection of sound waves is equal to the angle of incidence. This can be demonstrated using a watch as a source of sound, a board, a sheet of card or a large book as a reflecting surface, and two cardboard tubes through which we send the sound.

Hold the tubes as shown in the drawing. In front of the opening of one tube hold the ticking watch, and hold your ear against the open end of the other tube. The other ends of the tubes are a few inches away from the reflecting surface. By moving the tubes so that the angles which they make with the card alter, you will find that the sound of the watch is loudest and clearest when the tubes make equal angles with the

perpendicular to the card. This, then, demonstrates that the sound is reflected and that the angle of reflection is equal to the angle of incidence.

A remarkable demonstration of the reflection of sound can also be done with a radio or television set on which you can use the tone control to bring out the high notes. These highest notes, in fact, come out of the speaker in a fairly narrow conical beam. Go and sit to one side of the radio or television set and hold in front of the loudspeaker a piece of card, a 12-inch gramophone record in its sleeve or a large book. You will be able to play ball with the beam of high notes. When you sit beside the receiver you do not hear the high notes very well, but by means of a reflector you can hear them extremely well – quite astonishing.

Very strange is the way in which the inside of an umbrella reflects sound. Because of the concave shape the sound waves are reflected to a single point (in the same way that a concave mirror, as in a car headlamp, concentrates the rays of light). Hold your ear at that point, which lies on the handle of the umbrella, and you can hear the sounds from the world outside suddenly become much clearer. With two umbrellas you can even make the ticking of a watch audible across a distance of several yards. You can see how to do it in the drawing. Lay both umbrellas on the ground or on a table, and prop them up with suitably bent pieces of wire. Move your ear along the handle of one of the umbrellas until you reach the place where you hear sounds loudest. Fix a watch there with an elastic band. Now place your ear at the corresponding place at the other umbrella and you should be able to hear the watch – several yards away. The drawing shows how the waves of sound from the watch move and how they are reflected twice, before they arrive at your ear. It is most important that the axes (the handles) of your two umbrellas should be in the same straight line.

The dome of St Paul's Cathedral in London is famous for the way in which it acts as a great sound mirror. St Peter's in Rome is also well-known for its 'whispering gallery'. If someone speaks quite quietly at a certain point, the words can be heard quite clearly some distance away at a definite point.

28. Sound + sound = silence

You will need: tuning fork, or ordinary fork.

Is it possible that two sounds together make no sound? Yes, it is. Sound waves can be pictured as having alternate crests and troughs. If, therefore, the waves from two notes that are exactly similar in pitch and loudness, come together in such a way that the crests of one coincide exactly with the troughs of the other, the result is that the sound waves cancel one another out, so – silence.

As a matter of fact, as you remember, sound waves are a succession of compressions and rarefactions. If we start from there, then it is clear. If the compressions from one note coincide with the rarefactions from the other, the air remains undisturbed and no sound is heard.

You can demonstrate this phenomenon with a tuning fork or (less effectively) with an ordinary fork, preferably with two prongs. Strike the prongs of the

56

fork against a table, hold it upright on the table and slowly turn it round, at the same time holding your ear above it. You will observe that as the fork is rotated the sound is alternately loud and soft, and that there may be places where you cannot hear it at all. It is in these positions that the crests from one prong are coinciding with the troughs from the other. But strengthening of the sound can also occur: if the crests and troughs of one wave coincide with those of the other, the result is of course that we get higher crests and deeper troughs and consequently louder notes. Both circumstances arise because there are two sources of waves, one further away from the hearer than the other.

These phenomena occur not only with sound waves but also with electro-magnetic waves, such as light. Light plus light can produce darkness. And with radio waves too the waves can cancel each other out, reduce each other or reinforce each other. If you listen to very distant short-wave transmitters you sometimes have to put up with 'fading' – the sound is alternately loud and soft. This happens because the radio waves from one transmitter arrive at your aerial by different paths meeting in such a way that the waves either coincide with or oppose each other and so strengthen or weaken the signal. Such short waves do not reach your aerial directly over the surface of the earth but only after being reflected once or several times from a layer in the atmosphere, the so-called Heaviside-layer, which reflects radio waves. If this Heaviside-layer did not exist the modern world-wide radio traffic would be impossible.

29. High plus higher can be low

You will need: a few musical instruments, whistling kettle.

'High plus higher can be low' sounds like nonsense, doesn't it? But at first you were probably incredulous about the claim that 'sound plus sound gives silence' and are now convinced that under certain circumstances it is true. We are going to learn how another apparent impossibility is possible.

Stand near a whistling kettle in action and whistle a note of the same pitch. You hear only one note. Now gradually raise the pitch of your note. You may expect to hear two notes being whistled. That from your own whistling and that from the kettle. But you don't hear two, you hear three! A third one has appeared: a very low whistling note. Where has it come from? Not from your mouth. Not from the kettle. Well, then, where?

Suppose that the kettle whistles with a note of 500 vibrations per second. That is what you were doing at first, too. These two notes are heard as one. But as you whistle higher and reach notes of, say, 550, 570, 600 and 650 vibrations, then at the same time notes of 50, 70, 100, and 150 vibrations are heard. Their numbers of vibrations are the differences between the vibrations of the original notes, e.g. $570 - 500 = 70$. The source of these extra notes is the motion of the air particles in the waves of sound.

The kettle whistles a high note. You whistle a little higher. And now you hear a third, low note. So: high plus higher can be low. You can also produce these extra notes by whistling lower than the kettle. Whistle a note with, say, 430 vibrations a second, then a note of $500 - 430 = 70$ vibrations a second is produced.

Of course there are many other ways of causing these mysterious extra notes. For example, you can

whistle with a friend. Whistle the same note together first, and then one of you go up or down a little. Or one go up and the other go down, or both together go up or down by different amounts. You can also do this very well with two flutes or two violins, or two voices. It is quite startling when the extra note, which at first is too low to be heard, crosses the boundary of audibility and becomes audible as a very deep note. Then it is just as if a ghostly note has risen out of nothing.

If the pitches of two notes are only very slightly different, we hear the so-called 'beats', an alternate loudness and softness of the notes. Between two notes of, say, 500 and 502 vibrations a second there will be $502 - 500 = 2$ beats a second. With 504 and 500 there will be 4. The number of beats is obviously the difference between the two frequencies. A very important use is made of these extra notes and beats in music.

30. What causes the Doppler effect?

You will need: motor car or bicycle, whistle.

If you are going to be able to understand what is the cause of the Doppler Effect, you had better know what it is first. It is something very interesting. If you are travelling in a train and another train approaches whistling, no doubt you have noticed that the pitch of the whistle suddenly seems to drop. Yet there is no doubt that the whistle itself has carried on at the same pitch. You can observe a similar phenomenon if you are sitting in a car and another approaches sounding its horn. As the other car passes you, the pitch of the horn suddenly goes down. This is all quite easy to explain, but in order to do it we are going to have to exchange sound waves for people. A procession is

going along a street. Stand still at the beginning of the street, and one hundred people pass you in a minute. But if you walk along the street to meet these people many more will approach you in the course of a minute, maybe a hundred and fifty. If, on the other

hand, you walk slowly in the other direction the number of people who pass you is much less, perhaps seventy.

Now go to meet your approaching sound waves. You meet more in one second than if you stood still and so you hear more vibrations in a second: a higher note. On the other hand if you move away from the approaching sound waves you hear less in a second and so the note is lower. A hooting motor car, coming towards you goes away once it has passed you so that first you hear the horn higher and then lower. With a whistle, such as is used by football referees, and a bicycle you can observe the Doppler Effect quite easily. Get someone to stand still and blow the whistle

steadily, then you ride quickly towards and past him. You can hear the sound of the whistle first of all rising and then falling quite clearly.

The Doppler Effect occurs too with light waves and that makes it possible for the astronomers to establish the speed with which some of the nebulae are retreating from us. The fewer the number of light waves penetrating the eye per second the more does the colour of the light shift from the blue of the spectrum towards the red. This 'red-shift' can be measured very accurately and from it it is possible to calculate precisely the speed at which the nebulae are retreating from us, nebulae which are millions of light years away and are moving at speeds of tens of thousands of miles a second !

31. A gun for sound rings

You will need: round cardboard box with a bottom, piece of paper, pair of scissors, elastic band, candle.

There are people who can blow smoke rings, perfectly formed circles of smoke. With the aid of some very simple articles you too will be in a position to make such wonderful smoke rings for yourself. At the same time you will be able to produce a remarkable sound ring which will be able to extinguish a candle flame magically at a distance of several feet. Scientists have been able to carry out very many investigations with these sound rings. It is possible to produce in the air such powerful rings that a man has been knocked over some yards away. We are not going to risk anything like that, but our sound rings will be able to snuff a candle flame as quick as a flash at a distance that you could not cover by mere blowing.

Get a cardboard box (or tube closed at the end), cylindrical if possible, but if you can't manage this the largest cardboard cup available will do. If there is no lid or covering for the other end you can easily make one from stiff paper. In the centre of this lid cut a round hole, half an inch in diameter. Fasten the lid to the tube with gummed tape or an elastic band.

If you want to make smoke rings you will need some smoke. So you will have to ask someone who does

smoke to blow a few puffs of smoke in through the hole. If now you hold your smoke ring cannon horizontally and tap slowly on the bottom with a knuckle you will see beautiful smoke rings shoot out of the hole, holding their shape perfectly as they fly forwards.

You will be able to observe them to the best advantage if you illuminate them well with a lamp and view them against a dark background. And what do you see? In each of these rings the smoke is rolling round rapidly – a fantastic sight; it cannot be done in any other way.

Now for the destructive effect of the invisible sound rings which you can produce if you do not put any smoke in the tube but still tap on the bottom. Light a candle, aim your cannon towards the flame, tap once or twice on the bottom. Perhaps the flame only flickers a little, but if you aim correctly it is snuffed instantly by a sound ring. It is still possible even from more than three feet away.

Every spectator watching this will find it astonishing that just one flick of the finger against the bottom of the tube is sufficient to snuff the candle. The explanation is that in such a ring the air is revolving with such power and speed that the flame has to give in to a kind of miniature tornado.

32. A fountain in a glass case

You will need: large preserving jar, small bottle, cork, thin glass tube, or a transparent drinking straw, water, plate, damp paper.

You can make a fountain with a bottle fitted with a cork through which the thin glass tube passes. Fill the bottle three quarters full of water and stand it upright on a plate on a few sheets of damp paper. Now take the preserving jar and hold it for a while upside down over a burning candle or any other gentle flame so that the air inside gets thoroughly warm and expands so that some of it leaves the jar.

Now quickly put the jar over the small bottle and press it firmly down on to the damp paper. The air inside cools and contracts, reducing the pressure. The pressure of the air inside the bottle stays the same as it was before. It pushes the water out, up through the tube causing a pretty little fountain – a fountain inside the glass preserving jar.

33. The balloon and the bottle

You will need: bottle, party balloon, basin, warm water.

Blowing up such a small balloon, there's nothing to it, you say? But just try to blow it up inside a bottle. Push the balloon into the neck of the bottle with the aid of a pencil. Stretch the opening of the balloon back over the neck of the bottle and then blow. What looks so simple proves to be extremely difficult. No matter if you blow until you are red in the face the balloon only gets the very slightest bit bigger. Why?

The expansion of the balloon results in the air in the bottle having less space and so its pressure increases. Well, this pressure opposes the pressure you cause with your lungs until you cannot inflate the balloon any further.

So, a balloon cannot be blown up inside a bottle. But can a bottle blow up a balloon? Take the balloon from out of the bottle but stretch the opening over the neck again. Now stand the bottle in a basin of hot water, putting it in and taking it out several times gently so that there is no danger of the glass cracking. When the bottle is hot you can let it stay in the water. The heat makes the air in the bottle expand and so the pressure increases to more than the pressure outside. The result is that the balloon is blown up . . . by the bottle (or rather, by the air in the bottle).

34. From walking tumblers to Hovercraft

You will need: a few tumblers, hot water, draining board.

Have you ever noticed that tumblers when they are
stood upside down on the draining board after washing
up walk down it in the most odd way? It only happens
if the board is quite wet. What makes the glasses go
for a walk?

They are washed in hot water, so they are still
warm when they are put upside down on the draining
board. Thus the air inside the glasses gets warmed
and expands. A higher pressure is set up inside the
glasses which presses down on the water. Consequently, the glass is held up by a cushion of air; it
does not press down so heavily on the draining board,
but moves about freely on the thin film of water. It
can also happen that the air can escape in one direction with the result that the glass is pushed in the
opposite direction.

The smoother the surface the better do the glasses
walk. You may find this experiment works better in
the sink than on the draining board. Make sure that
there is a thin unbroken layer of water, hold the
glasses a bit longer than usual in water as hot as
possible – patience! – invert them and put them down
smartly so that they cool off as little as possible. Then
you will see how well they can walk. Sometimes they
don't simply walk . . . it is as though they were on
skates!

You may well ask yourself if this method of frictionless motion could not be used for transport. In fact it does happen in the Hovercraft, a British invention with a great future which can be used just as easily on the land as on water. In the Hovercraft a very strong blast of air is blown down under the vehicle so that a cushion of compressed air is formed and the Hovercraft does not actually touch the ground or the water. Forward motion is caused by a jet of air or of gases moving horizontally; created either by gas turbines or in some cases by propellers. The Hovercraft can not only move over the water at great speed, more than 60 miles per hour, but can also cross the coastline on to dry land. Vehicles based on the same principle, resting on a cushion of compressed air, will be ideal for the exploration and cultivation of marshy territory.

35. Waterdrops . . . skaters

You will need: metal sheet or pan, water, gas ring.

In the year 1755 a scientist named Leidenfrost described an experiment which is both well-known and fascinating and which we are now going to do.

Perhaps you have noticed that when a drop of water falls upon a red-hot plate it does not evaporate immediately but stays there sizzling for a little while or shoots away. It is worth while to observe this strange behaviour under the best possible conditions; so let us take a metal plate and lay it over a burning gas ring until it gets red hot. If you haven't got a gas ring you can use one of the hot plates on an electric cooker. A metal plate should be easy to find. You could use a lid from a large tin, an old saucepan or any thick piece of iron. Aluminium is liable to melt if you get it too hot. Whatever you do decide to use, make sure that it is quite clean first so that there is nothing left on it which can burn black.

When the plate is nice and hot, let a few drops of water fall on it. They do not boil away but stay sizzling, gliding over the surface swiftly or slowly, darting in all directions because of the slight irregularities on the surface of the plate. Many of them are just like competition skaters – you could imagine that you were at some display of championship skating.

How is it that these droplets do not boil away? The heat of the plate makes a little of the water under the drop evaporate and the steam which is formed acts as a cushion, not of air as in our previous experiment, but of steam. So between the drop and the hot plate there is a layer of steam which prevents the rest of the water from evaporating. The drop of water can now move about easily, quickly and free from friction, and it will do so as long as the plate is level enough.

A story is told of a workman in an iron foundry who was showing a visitor round. Wanting to impress the visitor the workman put his wet hand into some molten, white-hot iron without his hand being burnt. It is also well known that some men can walk across glowing red-hot stones or iron plates without any injury to their feet. How is all this possible? Possibly the answer is that the water on the hand or under the soles of the feet evaporates immediately and forms a protective cushion of steam around the hand or under the feet.

36. Blow a flame towards you

You will need: candle, 2 pieces of stiff paper or thin card, some gum or a paper-clip.

Everybody can blow a flame away from himself, or blow it out, that's child's play. But blow a flame towards you . . . yes, you can do that too, if you know how. But we need to know something about streamlining first. You know how important streamlining is in the design of cars and aircraft, a shape which reduces the resistance of the air as much as possible. Now the majority of people think that this shape is only important at the front because it is only the front which moves against the air. But this is not so – as we are going to demonstrate by blowing a flame towards us.

Light a candle, and hold between your mouth and the flame a square piece of card. Blow . . . and what do you see? The flame bends towards you? So there is a stream of air in your direction too. But how does that happen? All you did was blow a stream of air away from you.

The air which you blew out collided with the card and all kinds of eddies and whirlwinds were set up. The outcome of this was that a reduction of the pres-

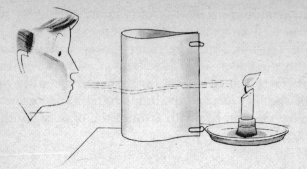

sure of the air behind the card was caused. But the surrounding air tries to restore the equilibrium and so it flows towards the region of lower pressure. Hence behind the card there is a stream of air which flows towards you. This is what makes the flame bend in your direction.

Now, if the back of a car or the back and sides of an aircraft are not well streamlined, when the car or air-craft is moving, streams of air flowing in the opposite direction may be set up. These air streams can have a braking effect. If you put between your mouth and the candle flame some object of a streamlined shape, you will see from the behaviour of the candle that the air can flow along almost unruffled. Bend a wide strip of paper round and fasten the two ends together with gum or a paperclip. Stand the paper on one of its curved edges, with the blunt curve towards you. Now when you blow, the flame goes back nicely and there are no opposing streams of air.

You come across some beautiful streamlined shapes in Nature – think of most birds and especially of the seagulls and the swallows, and of fish, for a good streamlined shape is important not only in the air but in water too.

37. Air resistance as a life saver

You will need: paper serviette, 4 pieces of thread, small doll.

As any cyclist will agree, the resistance of the air can be most annoying, but it can also be extremely useful. Were it not for the resistance of the air large hailstones would be able to strike us dead, and it is air resistance which has already saved thousands of lives by means of the parachute.

Shall we make a parachute? We can use a paper serviette. To each of the corners tie a piece of thread about a foot long. On to these four threads fasten a small, strong but flexible plastic doll such as you can buy in any toy-shop. Or you can make yourself a doll from modelling clay, or just use a small weight.

Then let your parachute make a test flight. Stand on a chair, hold the paper serviette firmly in the centre and then let go. Your parachute floats slowly to the floor. Whatever you hang on your parachute must not be too heavy, nor on the other hand too light. You must find out by experiment which weight is the best. Get your friends to make parachutes too, and organize competitions to find out whose parachute can stay in the air longest. If the wind is not too strong you can let your parachutes fall from an upstairs window.

Make experiments with larger parachutes, made with stronger paper or a good piece of nylon material, the stuff that real parachutes are made with. The balance of your parachute can be improved if you make a small hole in the centre of it. Then you will get a smoother descent with far less swinging about.

38. Fly a 'slow roll'

You will need: sheet of stiff paper.

Many years ago now I was taken up stunt flying by the well-known, but alas now dead, test pilot Gerben Sonderman van Fokker. In a two-seater aircraft, a Harvard Trainer, Sonderman flew all kinds of figures, including several times looping the loop, a 'falling leaf' (in which our plane went down just like an autumn leaf) and also the famous 'slow roll'. In this the plane flies horizontally, turning slowly round a horizontal axis, and I saw the ground (Holland) alternately above and below me – a wonderful sensation.

An aeroplane made from a folded piece of paper can make slow rolls too, turning round on its axis in flight. Fold a sheet of paper as is shown in the drawing. In this way you can make a paper glider which will perform very well. It is a good idea to gum the sides of the main fold together.

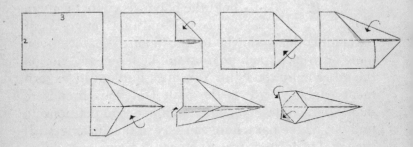

How do you make the glider perform a slow roll? Quite simply: by folding the end of one wing upwards and the end of the other down (see the sketch). How much you must bend the wings can only be decided by experiment. In any case it is less than a right angle. Bending one wing down and the other wing up results in a downward pull on one side and an upward thrust on the other, causing the glider to rotate round its axis as it flies. Such a pair of forces producing circular motion is known as a 'couple'.

39. Make your own gasworks

You will need: long-stemmed clay pipe, some clay, small pieces of coal.

If you own a long-stemmed clay pipe (and they can still be bought) you can make your own gasworks which will work in the same way as the large gasworks in the town. Get some small pieces of coal – if necessary break some up with a hammer – and put them in the bowl of the pipe. Now seal off the bowl and make it airtight with some clay. Put the bowl of the pipe in the fire or over a strong gas flame so that the coal gets strongly heated. After a while, hold a lighted match or taper near the stem of the pipe and a flame may appear – a real gas flame produced by the 'dry distillation' (strong heating in the absence of air) of the coal.

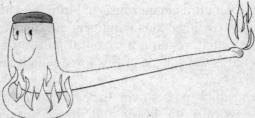

If you can't get hold of a clay pipe you can put your pieces of coal in a strong test tube closed off with a cork fitted with a glass tube. You will be able to get a small flame at the end of the glass tube.

40. Aeroplane wing . . . fly!

You will need: pencil, piece of stiff paper, pair of scissors, paste or gum, vacuum cleaner.

How does an aeroplane fly? How is it that such a heavy object can rise in the air? We can demonstrate this by making a piece of a wing. Bend a strip of stiff paper as is shown in the drawing and stick the two ends together. If you make the underside flat or slightly hollow and the upperside well rounded – as in the drawing – you will have a section of an aeroplane wing.

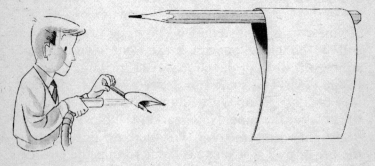

Hang the wing over a pencil as shown in the drawing and blow against the blunt end. (For this, it is much more convenient and far less tiring to use the hose of the vacuum cleaner inserted into the end which blows.) You will see the wing section turn upwards round the pencil, reach a horizontal position and stay there. What is the source of this force which keeps the wing horizontal?

The air which passes over the wing takes the same time to pass over the lower and upper surfaces from front to back. But the air passing over the arched upper surface has to travel a greater distance. This means that the air over the upper surface must move faster than the air underneath. There is a scientific law called Bernouilli's Law (which we shall investigate in a later experiment) which states: the faster a gas moves, the lower is its pressure. So the pressure of the air above the wing is lower than it is beneath, and thus the wing is forced upwards. In this way an aeroplane gets the major part of its lifting power.

The airscrews or jet engines of an aeroplane pull or push it so fast forwards that the necessary opposite wind, the fast air stream against the wings, is caused.

41. The wonderful story of a drop of water

Not long ago I told Tirtsa, my travel-loving eight-year-old daughter, that if she were a drop of water and not a little girl she would be able to make really long journeys. First of all she might swim around, along with other drops of water, in the wide ocean. After a while, however, she would evaporate in the heat of the sun's rays and in the form of invisible vapour soar up into the blue sky. Then one night, when it was bitterly cold, the vapour would condense around a floating speck of dust and she would take on her original form again, a drop of water.

Together with millions of other drops of water, Tirtsa would now become part of something that looks like an enormous mountain of pink foam in the beams of the rising sun – but which is in reality a cloud. High above the waves, this cloud drifts over to dry land like a stately galleon in full sail. Tirtsa would float above white surf, a sandy beach, lovely green hills, meadows and woods and here and there the gay red roofs of a village. . . .

'What would happen then, Daddy?' Tirtsa asked, intrigued.

'Nothing for the time being, my child. As long as the wind, temperature and degree of dampness remain unchanged, you'll drift across strange lands for a day or two in that ball of cotton-wool. But clouds only have a temporary existence and sooner or later they either turn into vapour if it's very warm or they change into rain, snow or hail. What would happen to you during the next few months would depend on the sort of downfall and where you landed. Take my advice, be careful not to drift amongst high mountains. For that could mean a hold-up of many decades and you're someone who likes travelling! There in a high ridge of mountains it's very likely that you would crystallize into snow or hail, fall, be buried deep under other snow and become part of the ice of a glacier, a thick tongue of ice perhaps a mile long and a hundred yards thick, which takes decades to slide down extremely slowly, then melt and join a mountain stream which flows out into a river. . . .

77

'And what happens if you should fall in the form of rain, snow, or hail on lower lying land? Well, then there are many possibilities. A cow might drink you up, or a sparrow or a human being. Or you might be sucked up by a plant. You might evaporate in the sun. You could sink down deep into the earth and arrive in an underground stream where it's very dark. That wouldn't be very pleasant. Therefore, dear child, my advice to you is to fall somewhere where the surplus water is drained away by ditches and brooks. Then you'll make the pleasantest of journeys through charming landscapes and you can be more or less certain of eventually going into a river. . . .'

'And then?' Tirtsa asked. 'Must I swim all the way down that river?'

'No, of course not. You just float along with it, downstream, until you come to the sea into which nearly all rivers flow. You become part of the world's seas and oceans again. You've arrived back where you started. You've made a round trip, which we call the water cycle and you can start on the round trip again. For water on our earth never stops repeating this cycle. It rises out of the sea by evaporating, it forms clouds in the sky, it falls back into the sea as rain, snow or hail, or it falls on land, runs into a river, and flows back into the sea. And then it repeats this cycle again by evaporating and condensing, time after time, for ever and for ever. . . .'

Another circular story

'What fun that your story ended where it began,' Tirtsa said. 'Do you know another story that ends where it begins and that's also about water and rain? Go on, do tell me another story with the same sort of cycle in it!'

And then I told Tirtsa the beautiful as well as

philosophical fable of the Japanese stonemason, which has been recounted by a writer who called himself 'Multatuli' (*much have I borne*) because he had been through so much suffering.

'Once upon a time there was a man who hewed stones out of rock. His work was heavy and he laboured hard, but his wages were small and he was not content. Therefore, he sighed and cried, "Oh to be rich and rest upon cushions of red silk!" And an angel appeared from heaven and said, "Your wish shall be granted." And he was rich and rested upon cushions of red silk. But one day the king of the land rode past on a snowwhite steed, escorted by many horsemen. When the rich man perceived this, it saddened him that he could not ride in such a manner. He sighed deeply and cried, "Would that I were king!"

'And an angel appeared from heaven and said, "Your wish shall be granted." And he was king. In magnificent apparel, he rode on his snow-white steed accompanied by many horsemen before him and after him. But the sun blazed down and scorched the earth so that the grass withered. And the king complained that the sun was burning his face and was therefore mightier than he. And he was not content. He sighed deeply and cried, "Would that I were the sun!"

'And an angel appeared from heaven and said, "Your wish shall be granted." And he was the sun. And he sent his beams up above and down below, to the right side and to the left side and all round about. And he scorched the grass of the earth and the faces of kings. Then a cloud came between him and the earth and the beams of the sun were stopped by the

cloud. And he was angry that his power had been challenged and he complained that the cloud was mightier than he. And he was not content. He desired to be a cloud that had so much power.

'And an angel appeared from heaven and said, "Your wish shall be granted." And he became a cloud and went between the sun and the earth and intercepted the beams so that the grass turned green. The cloud rained large drops upon the earth and caused the rivers to rise and floods destroyed the fields and villages. And he fell upon a rock which did not yield. And he splashed down upon it in angry streams, but still the rock did not yield. And he became wrathful because the rock would not yield and because the rock was mightier than he. And he was not content. He cried, "That rock is mightier than I. I wish to be that rock!"

'And an angel appeared from heaven and said, "Your wish shall be granted!" And he turned into rock and was unyielding when it rained. Then there came a man with a pickaxe and hewed stone out of the rock. And the rock said, "What is this, that this man is mightier than I and hews stone out of my very lap?" And he was not content. He cried, "I am weaker than this man. Therefore I wish to be this man!"

'And an angel appeared from heaven and said, "Your wish shall be granted." And he was a stone-mason. And he hewed stones out of rock and he laboured hard for small wages and he was content. . . .'

Liquid of life

Water is as indispensable to life on earth as blood is to our bodies. Blood, for that matter, is 99% water, and our whole body more than 90% water. Two-thirds of the earth's surface is covered with water, the commonest of all substances in this world and at the same time the most versatile. For instance, in how many different ways do we use it in our homes? We drink it if we are thirsty and we make tea and coffee with it. We wash ourselves, our crockery, our clothes and much more besides in it. We rinse all sorts of un-pleasant things away with it. We water our plants, we cook our food in it.

Water was the cradle of life. For it was in water more than a thousand million years ago that the wonder of the reproduction of groups of molecules took place. This was the first form of life on earth. It was the sea which of old played host to many forms of life and in which a large part of the evolution to more highly developed forms of life took place. It is the sea with its warm streams which, like an enormous central heating system, provides Western Europe with such a mild climate. It was by sea the explorers sailed to dis-cover the largest part of the globe. World trade is carried on by means of the sea. And what is that sea? Water. . . .

Water is of more value than gold to the thirsty in the desert. All living nature quenches its thirst with water! It is from water, combined with air and salts dissolved in water, that all plants are made. And without those plants as food neither the animal world nor we ourselves could exist! Our human body is made up of air, salts and . . . water!

Thousands of years ago the oldest civilizations were to be found where the water of rivers led to great fertility and provided good means of transport. This was along the Euphrates and the Tigris in Mesopotamia, the Nile in Egypt, the Indus in India and the Yangtse-Kiang in China.

Without water there would be no swimming, no skating, no ski-ing, no rowing or sailing. Without water there would be no hydro-electricity, no smooth lakes, no rushing waterfalls, no colourful rainbow. Without water there would be no angling and no fish and chips, no splashing fountains and no diving. But this is a somewhat superfluous list, for without water there wouldn't be any life and we wouldn't exist. So let's end this short tribute to water with the clear-cut statement that water is a chemical compound, each molecule of which consists of two atoms of hydrogen and one atom of oxygen so that the formula is H_2O. Water appears as a solid, a liquid and in the form of vapour; it is odourless and tasteless and very faintly bluish in colour; it reacts neutrally; it can freeze at a pressure of one atmosphere at $0°C$ and can boil at $100°C$ – and any arguments to the contrary will not hold water.

42. A waterpipe from . . . wool or cotton threads

You will need: 2 glasses or jam jars, woollen or cotton threads.

Waterpipes? Surely they're made from metal or plastic tubes, not woollen or cotton threads! How can water run through the fluff which is found around the seeds of the cotton plant?

Get two glasses or jam jars. Set one of them about eight inches higher than the other. In the upper one let a length of thick cotton or woollen thread hang,

with the other end lying on the bottom of the empty glass. The upper end must also touch the bottom of the higher glass. If you have only thin thread, twist two pieces together to make a thicker one. Now fill the upper glass with water. You will see the lower, empty glass gradually fill with water, via the pipe made of cotton or wool.

If you go away for a few days, you can use cotton threads to make sure that your plants have enough water during your absence. Get a good-sized pan, bucket or basin and set it up somewhere above your plants. If you now arrange woollen or cotton threads from the pan to the plants, they will be kept watered automatically.

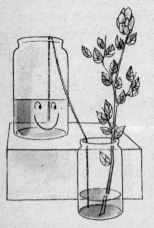

How does it work? It works by the capillary action of thin tubes. If you stand a thin glass tube or a thin straw in water, the water rises a short way up the tube (and a little higher at the sides than at the centre of the tube). This happens because the molecules of the glass or straw and those of the water attract each other. The thinner the tube, the higher the water rises because of the capillary action. In our everyday lives this capillary rise plays quite an important role. Cotton consists of very fine tubes, and so it is able to 'suck' up the water or, for instance, paraffin through the wick of an oil-stove. Similarly the wick of a candle soaks up the liquid wax. The fine tubes of blotting paper soak up the ink, and towels, teacloths and bandages absorb liquids so well simply because of capillary action.

Nature gives us the most outstanding example of capillary action. Plants and trees are able to take up water from the earth largely because of the capillary action of very fine tubes in the roots, stem and branches.

Very fascinating indeed is the capillary action of sugar. Hold a lump of sugar with one corner in coffee or tea and you will see the liquid quickly rise up into the lump.

43. The drop of a coin

You will need: bottle, sixpence, match, water.

On top of an open bottle lay a match which has been broken, or cracked, but not separated into two pieces. It should be in the shape of a 'V'. Lay the coin on top of the cracked match. Now you must ask someone if he can possibly make the coin fall into a bottle without his touching the coin, the match or the bottle. This will make him scratch his head. . . .

Now you go into action. Dip your finger into water, take it out and let the droplets fall on the place where the match is cracked. By capillary action the woody fibres take up the water, which makes them swell, and now what happens? The two halves of the match widen out, the V opens and eventually the ends are so far apart that the coin is not supported any longer. Then the scientific experiment is concluded by the drop of a coin.

The force produced by the swelling of the dampened wood fibres is so great that it can split the heaviest blocks of stone. The ancient Egyptians made use of it four thousand years ago when they needed thousands of blocks of stone of about a cubic yard. In quarries by the Nile they used to cut grooves in the rocks which they wanted to split. Then they would bore holes in the grooves, drive close-fitting wedges into the holes with hammers and finally pour water over the wedges. This made the wood swell with so much force that the rocks were split along the grooves.

44. Capillarity again

You will need: 2 sheets of glass, basin of water, ink, match, elastic band.

There is a law in science which says that in open vessels which are joined together, the surface of a liquid always lies in a horizontal plane. But this is no longer true if the vessels are narrow tubes. In this case, because of the great attraction between the molecules of the liquid and those of the sides of the tubes, the liquid creeps up the tube – by capillary action.

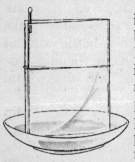

You can demonstrate this capillary rise of a liquid very nicely by using two small sheets of glass. Make them very clean by washing them well in hot water. Lay a match between them along one pair of edges and hold the opposite edges as close together as possible by putting a rubber band round them. Now hold them upright in water coloured with a little red or blue ink. You will see the water rising highest where the plates are closest together. There the layer of water is thinnest, and thus lightest, and so the capillary action is able to raise it highest.

45. Make a siphon

You will need: 2 glasses or jam jars, water, piece of rubber tubing.

You can have a lot of pleasure from a piece of rubber tubing about eighteen inches long. Of course you can make a fountain by pushing one end over a tap and pointing the other end upwards. But you can also make a siphon from it. How? Quite simply. Stand two glasses or jam jars, half-filled with water, side by side. Let the tubing hang down, and with your finger close the lower end. Now fill the tube with water. Close the upper end with another finger and place each end into one of the glasses, below the water, then take your fingers away. Raise one of the glasses a little, and you will see the surface of the water slowly sinking because water flows out of it into the other glass. Now you will notice something strange: the water-levels in both glasses or jars are both exactly the same. As long as the two surfaces are not on the same level – in a horizontal plane – the water will flow through your siphon. When the flow stops, the water-levels in both glasses are the same.

How does it happen? There is a scientific law which says that in the same liquid with the same horizontal surfaces the pressures are equal – the law of Hydrostatics. Air pressure plays no part in this, because it is the same on each of the two water surfaces in our glasses. Now take a look at the second drawing: at the level of B a higher column of water presses than on the same level of water in A, so the pressure on B is greater. This situation cannot continue. Hence the water indicated by H, presses down the water beneath it until the surfaces in both glasses are the same.

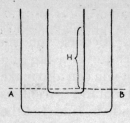

This is why in vessels joined together – communicating vessels – the liquid surfaces are at the same level. The water gauge used on steam engines works on this principle, and so do water supply systems in which the water is kept in a high reservoir or water-tower. A rubber tube such as you have been using as a siphon is a very convenient way of changing the water in an aquarium without disturbing the fish too much.

46. Which hole will win?

You will need: empty tin (e.g. large syrup tin such as the school canteen uses), sharp nail.

No, this race is not as exciting as a horse race, for if you use your brains you know very well which hole will win.

Down the side of the tin make a series of holes along a slanting line. Now, if you put the tin under a tap, well above the sink, and let the water run into it, from which hole will the water run the fastest, that is, with the most force? If you choose the top one, you will be hopelessly wrong, because the jet from the bottom hole is the strongest by a long way. The next hole above spouts not quite as far, and the top hole spouts the shortest distance of them all. The water spouts out of the hole because of the pressure of the water above the hole. The higher the column of water above the hole, the heavier it is and so the greater pressure it can exert. So the jet of water from a lower hole has more force than one higher up.

47. A water scale

You will need: rubber hot water bottle or strong plastic bag, rubber tube about 5 feet long, 2 pieces of glass tube, one 6 inches and the other 2 feet long, large cork.

Make a personal weighing machine for only a few pence – is that possible? This is how you can do it. Along a cupboard or doorpost fix a rubber tube with a glass tube pushed into the upper end. The lower end of the tube is connected to the cork, which has had a hole bored through it to take a short length of glass tube. Half-fill the bottle with water and push the cork in hard (it must fit very tightly, with no leakage whatever).

Lay a small board on top of the bottle or bag. If somebody stands on the plank you will expect that his weight will force all the water out of the bag, up the rubber tube and out of the glass tube at the top. But this does not happen. In fact, some of the water rises up the tube, but stops at a certain height – clearly visible in the glass tube. How does that happen? A thin column of water in the rubber tube, weighing only a few ounces, balancing a person weighing, probably, nearly a hundred pounds?

It is explained by Pascal's Law, which states: the pressure in a liquid is transmitted equally in all directions. If the rubber tube has an area of cross-section of $\frac{1}{4}$ square inch and the hot water bottle a surface area of 80 square inches, then a force of $\frac{1}{4}$ pound weight in the column of water exerts a pressure of $\frac{1}{4} \div \frac{1}{4} = 1$ lb. wt./sq. in. and produces a force of $80 \times 1 = 80$ pounds weight. That is the same as the weight of the person on the bottle.

In practice it is not necessary to measure the area of the bottle and the diameter of the rubber tube accurately. But we mark out our scale by getting several people to weigh themselves first on a conventional scale. Suppose that we have, for example, three people of 96 lbs., 110 lbs. and 124 lbs., we then get them to stand, in turn, on the board. On a piece of paper, behind the glass tube, we can mark the level of the water for each person. Then it is fairly easy to mark out a scale in divisions of two pounds. In this way we can make ourselves quite an accurate scale for practically no cost.

Hydraulic weighing machines constructed on this principle are often used for weighing very heavy objects.

48. Oil and vinegar from the same bottle

You will need: bottle with a cork, salad oil, vinegar.

Almost eighty years ago there appeared a book *Entertaining Science* by Tom Tit, the pen-name of Arthur Good (although he sounds English he wrote in French). The following story appeared in the book: You are on a picnic with a happy party of friends on a sunny day, somewhere in the country. Each one has brought his share of the food, and there is great excitement as it is being unpacked. But all at once everyone looks worried. The host, or leader, who was to provide the salad, has done it all right; but the oil and vinegar are in the same bottle! 'Keep calm,' says one of the guests, 'it will be all right!' The bottle is handed to him and he can see, of course, two clearly separated liquids, the oil with its lower density floating on top of the vinegar. Without shaking it, he goes round the group and pours out on to each plate just as much oil and vinegar as each one wants!

How did he manage it? Well, you can try it for yourself by pouring first vinegar and then salad oil into a small bottle. If you choose oil, then very carefully tilt the bottle so that only oil runs out. To pour out vinegar, put the cork in, slowly invert the bottle without shaking it so that the denser vinegar comes into the neck of the bottle. Pull the cork out a little way so that a small jet of vinegar can run out. So you can see how, from one bottle, oil or vinegar can be poured at will.

49. A liquid tricolour

You will need: glass tube, methylated spirits or alcohol, oil, water, coloured ink or watercolour, cork.

Many countries have flags which are not as complicated as the Union Jack or the Stars and Stripes, but simply consist of three stripes of different colours. Examples are the flags of Holland and France, red, white and blue. A three-coloured flag like these is known as a tricolour. Let us make a liquid tricolour.

Get one of those glass tubes in which tablets are sometimes sold. Wash it well and take the label off. Fill the tube to one third of its depth with water. Add a drop or two of red ink so that the water is coloured. Gently pour in enough oil, cycle oil for instance, to fill the second third of the tube. Notice that the oil and the water do not mix. On top of the oil carefully pour some methylated spirits coloured blue with more ink. Close the tube securely with a cork or stopper and your liquid tricolour is ready!

Because the oil is less dense than water it stays on the top. Methylated spirit (or alcohol) is less dense than oil and so it floats on top of that.

Now you can turn the flag upside down? Yes: if you do it very slowly and carefully. At first it looks as though your flag is ruined, as if the colours have run together. But you will see the methylated spirits come on top again and the red water underneath. And this is quite in order, for the water is the densest and the methylated spirits the least dense.

50. Waterproof bandage?

You will need: milk bottle, old nylon stocking, piece of gauze bandage, elastic band, water.

Is a bandage waterproof? A stupid question you say, because obviously the water passes through all those holes. That's what you think. We will show you the opposite. And we are going to make a valve, a valve for water!

A valve is something like a mousetrap: you can get in all right but you cannot get out again. A valve means: a one-way road. A well-known example is the valve in a cycle or car tyre. The air can go in, but it cannot get out.

Our water-valve consists of a piece of an old nylon stocking. With the help of an elastic band fasten it across the mouth of a milk bottle. Can we fill the bottle now? Well, try. Hold the bottle under the tap, and let the water fall on the nylon fabric. The water goes straight through. Yes, it looks as though there is a big hole in the nylon, because the water goes through so easily.

But when the bottle is full and you turn it upside down it seems as though the light nylon material with all its holes has suddenly become impassable to water. For not a drop falls out – the water stays in just as the air stays in a bicycle tyre. A perfect valve.

But how does it happen?

Patience! First of all we are going to try it again with a piece of gauze bandage. And we find that the gauze, which is very light, made of thin threads loosely interwoven, holds the water back too.

Now again, how does it all happen? By two phenomena: air pressure and the surface tension of the water. Against every square inch of the gauze over the

neck of the bottle there is an outside force of fourteen and a half pounds. So that there is a force of about that amount on the piece you are using. This force is more than enough to support the water in the bottle.

Then there is the surface tension of the water; this property of liquids causes the surface to behave like an elastic skin. This happens because the molecules in the surface layer are very strongly attracted by the molecules in the layer underneath, but not by the molecules of the air above. The top layer of molecules experiences a force towards the interior of the liquid and so behaves like a stretched sheet. You can demonstrate this easily by laying very carefully on the surface a razor blade or a needle. Although iron is seven times denser than water, the razor blade and the needle float on the surface – thanks to the surface tension. This is why pondskaters and many other insects can run about on the water without getting their feet wet. The surface tension of water drops is quite high and so the fabric of umbrellas and raincoats is able to repel water.

To return to our milk bottle: because the surface of the water acts like a skin, and the air presses with a force of many pounds, the water cannot pass through the nylon or the gauze – they are waterproof! You can pour water *in* quite easily because the gauze is so thin, and there is room for the air to come out past the entering stream of water.

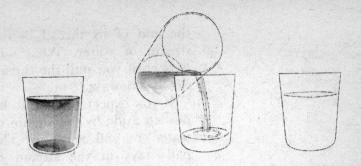

51. A sea change

You will need: a glass, water, ink, bleach.

Fill a glass with water and add a few drops of blue ink, enough to make the water deep blue, but no more than absolutely necessary. Now what would you say if you were to pour the blue liquid into another glass and the blue colour disappeared without a trace, leaving the liquid as clear as water once again? Magic? Not a bit of it! Only a bit of chemistry, and a little bleach.

If you are going to show this astonishing experiment to your friends there is no need to mention this but on the bottom of the empty glass put a few drops of bleach. Pour into it the water which you have coloured blue with the ink, and the blue substance is converted into another colourless compound by the chlorine in the bleach. It may be necessary to stir or shake the glass a little, but if you have used as little ink as possible and have added just the right amount of bleach, then pour smartly and the blue should disappear as if by magic!

52. The strange antics of a table tennis ball

You will need: table tennis ball, cellulose tape, piece of thread, water tap, vacuum cleaner.

Fasten the piece of thread to the table tennis ball with a bit of cellulose tape so that the ball can hang freely. Turn the tap on and let the ball hang on

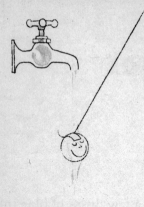

the end of its thread in the stream of water. What will happen if you pull the thread slowly sideways?

If you expect the ball to be pushed aside by the stream of water you will be wrong. The ball stays in the stream of water – even though the force of gravity – the weight of the ball – is pulling it down and the force of the stream of water is coming from above. The ball stays caught in the stream — apparently contradicting all logic and the laws of nature.

'Apparently', because the ball is really obeying the scientific law discovered by the Swiss, Bernouilli, which states: if the speed of a liquid or gas increases, then the pressure inside that liquid or gas decreases. In the fast-moving water there is a lower pressure than in the surrounding air, which is stationary. Therefore the air, whose pressure is greater, pushes the ball into the region of lower pressure – the stream of water.

Direct the air from a vacuum cleaner hose upwards and put a table tennis ball into the jet of air. You can take the thread off the ball. The ball floats in the jet because there is a lower pressure in the fast-moving upward stream of air than in the air around it. So the surrounding air always pushes the ball into the jet. In the water experiment, too, though the force of the running tapwater is quite strong the pressure is lower than in the surrounding air. This experiment, therefore, is one that can be carried out in both wet and dry conditions.

Heat

53. Expansion by heat

You will need: steel knitting needle or metal curtain rod, cork, 2 pins, 2 drinking glasses, candle.

Most things expand when they are heated. This explains the action of a thermometer, of which we are going to make a model in our next experiment. This expansion by raising the temperature can be very troublesome in large metal objects, for example bridges and railway lines. For this reason rails are never laid closely end to end, but a small gap is left between them, as otherwise on a hot day they would buckle and nasty accidents could be caused.

The expansion due to a rise in temperature is only very small, so small that we cannot see it in a knitting needle or piece of curtain rail. But we can demonstrate that they get longer when they are heated. Push a steel knitting needle or a piece of curtain rod through a cork. Stick pins into the sides of the cork at opposite ends of a diameter and let the whole lot rest on the bottoms of two upturned glasses. Adjust the position of the needle in the cork so that it remains horizontal.

Now place a lighted candle under one half of the needle. That part expands, becomes longer, and upsets the equilibrium so that it tilts downwards.

Take the candle away; that half of the needle cools down again and the needle returns to its horizontal position. Put the candle under the other side, and that side gets longer and tilts down. So, by moving the candle from one side to the other and back you can make your needle move slowly up and down like a seesaw.

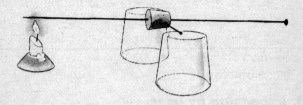

54. Make a thermometer
You will need: bottle, cork, drinking straw, water, coloured ink.

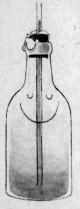

Just to remind you: in general, when a thing is heated it expands. This is the principle of the thermometer. As the temperature in the bulb of mercury rises, the mercury expands and rises higher in the narrow glass tube. The thermometer which we are going to make cannot be expected to register the temperature very accurately, but it will show you how a thermometer works.

Fill a bottle completely with water which you have coloured with some ink. Push into the neck a cork through which you have bored a hole, so that the straw will fit in it. It is not easy to bore a hole in a cork, because the cork tends to close up again. One of the best ways of doing it is to burn a hole through the cork with a red-hot knitting needle or nail. Hold the red-hot needle or nail in a pair of pliers. Now it is essential that straw, cork and bottle fit together so well that no air can get in or out. You can make a very good hermetic seal by dropping some melted candle wax on the cork or pushing some modelling clay or chewing gum on to it.

By pressing down on the cork of the full bottle you can make some of the water rise a little way up the straw. Now put the bottle into a pan of hot water standing on the stove or on a radiator. The water in the bottle expands and the surface of the water in the straw rises. If the bottle is allowed to cool, the water goes down, and so we see that the height of the water depends upon the temperature. So we have been able to demonstrate in a very simple way the principle of the thermometer.

55. A sawdust roundabout

You will need: bottle of water, some sawdust, stove or radiator.

Fill a bottle almost to the top with water. Shake some sawdust gently in the water so that it no longer floats but mixes well with the water. Now, is it possible to make the sawdust move from below to the top and from the top to the bottom without touching the bottle?

Yes, if you get to work in a certain way. How? By putting the bottle on a warm stove or radiator. What happens when the bottom of the bottle gets warm? The water at the bottom of the bottle becomes warmer and thus less dense than the cooler water above it. Therefore the warm water rises and the unheated, cooler and denser water sinks down. The result is a continuous circulation of the water, because as the cooler water sinks and gets warmed, it becomes lighter than the previously warmed water which has by now cooled down a little and has become a little heavier. The water therefore continues to circulate, taking the sawdust with it. You cannot see the movement of the water itself but you can certainly see how the sawdust is carried round. At first slowly, but soon faster, it goes round and round and up and down, a fascinating sight – a visible demonstration that the water circulates.

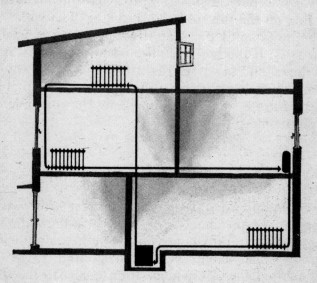

This is made use of in central heating systems. The water is heated in a boiler in the lower part of the house; it gets lighter and rises by itself to radiators placed higher up, while the water which has cooled down returns to the boiler. In this way, in many central heating systems the water circulates without the aid of a pump.

56. Why is this candle hollow?

You will need: glass of water, candle, nail or screw.

When I was a boy I used to stay at my grandmother's, and at bedtime I used to go up to bed with a candlestick: a burning candle in an enamelled metal candleholder fixed to a flat plate which had a handle. Candles can so easily cause fires and so Grandmother always used to warn me to be very careful.

In past times all sorts of devices were used to try to reduce the danger of fire from candlesticks, for example, by letting a candle float in a glass of water. Let us do it too. Stick a nail or screw into the bottom of a candle to weight it, and place in a tumbler or jam jar full of water. Only a small amount of the floating candle remains above the water. Maybe you will have to use a smaller nail or screw. Light the candle.

Now, here's something remarkable: the candle burns hollow. In other words, at the top it gets more and more concave. This happens because the wax at the top is cooled so much by the water that it cannot melt and so cannot be burned by the wick. Now, if you show the hollow candle to your friends later, not one of them will be able to make out how the candle came to be hollowed out so neatly. Believe me, when the floating candle is almost burnt out, it is a fascinating sight, this super-hollow candle!

57. Cooling by evaporation

You will need: thermometer (not a clinical thermometer), a little methylated spirit, rag.

Heat is necessary for the evaporation of a liquid, and the liquid extracts the heat it needs from its surroundings. You can observe this very clearly if you put a few drops of methylated spirit on your hand and then blow across it. The blowing speeds up the rate of evaporation of the 'meths', but the meths needs heat in order to evaporate. It takes the heat from your hand and so your hand feels cold.

Hold the bulb of a thermometer in a few drops of meths in the hollow of your hand, and then blow. The mercury in the thermometer drops. You can also wrap a rag soaked in meths around the bulb and blow on it. As you blow, the heat necessary for the evaporation is taken from the glass of the thermometer which then cools down. Instead of meths you can use eau-de-cologne, or even water. If you wet your finger with water and then blow on it you can feel your finger getting cold.

Our bodies make use of the fact that heat is necessary for evaporation and that it can be taken from its surroundings. If you get very hot, you sweat. If there is enough wind the dampness of the perspiration evaporates very rapidly and your skin cools down. When use is made of fans or ventilators to provide cooling, and artificial wind is made to hasten the evaporation. The current of air from the fan is not itself cool, but it makes the evaporation take place more rapidly and so causes cooling.

All refrigerators depend on the cooling caused by evaporation. In refrigerators use is made of a liquid which evaporates easily, usually a liquid known as Freon. In order to evaporate, the Freon extracts heat from its surroundings and so the refrigerator gets cold. The evaporated Freon is liquefied again by compressing it with a motor-driven pump. The heat which is set free by the compression is carried away by air passing over a ventilator. The compressed and cooled Freon vapour condenses back to liquid Freon which fills the circulating system. This Freon evaporates again, extracts heat from the refrigerator, so that the contents are cooled, and so the process goes on.

Some refrigerators work by burning gas or oil. In these cases, strange as it may seem, the heat of the flame is converted indirectly into cold. The heat of the flame produces the high pressure which is necessary for the conversion of the gaseous Freon into a liquid again and makes the Freon circulate. Refrigerators of this type, known as absorption refrigerators, have the advantage that they contain no moving parts and so wear less, and are quite silent. But their consumption of gas or oil makes them dearer to run than electric machines with a motor and a pump, the type known as compression refrigerators.

58. Colder with soda and hypo

You will need: some soda or hypo, glass with a thin bottom, spoon, piece of card, thermometer (not clinical).

Have you ever noticed that if you take a handful of soda crystals and hold them under a dripping tap so that the water drips on them your hand becomes quite cold? Soda and water are an example of a cooling mixture. Soda needs heat in order to be able to dissolve in water. The soda takes this heat from the water and so the mixture becomes colder than either of the two substances was beforehand.

With a thermometer you can follow the fall in temperature while it happens. Put into a glass just enough water to cover the bulb of a thermometer, then add a few spoonfuls, or a handful, of soda crystals and stir the mixture with the thermometer. If it reads, say, 16° C (60° F), the temperature can fall as low as 10° C (50° F).

Hypo has a much better cooling effect. It is the salt used in photography for fixing and its real name is sodium thiosulphate. If you stand a thin-bottomed glass on a piece of wet card, pour a little cold water into the glass and then quickly stir in some hypo, it is quite likely that the glass will freeze to the cardboard. In any case, you can detect quite a large degree of cooling just by holding the glass in your hand. Even more effective is the freezing mixture made with ammonium nitrate and water.

Perhaps some summer day you want to cool your lemonade down a few degrees and you have no ice available, but there is some soda. Put the glass of lemonade into a larger glass containing some soda crystals. Pour water over the crystals and stir the water to dissolve the soda. Wait a few minutes and soon you will be able to enjoy your nice cool drink.

59. Make your own ice-cream

You will need: some snow, cooking salt, large pan, small aluminium pan, spoon, water or milk, sugar and flavouring, flour.

When there is snow lying about you can take the opportunity to make yourself some ice-cream by mixing snow with cooking salt (you don't eat this but use it as a freezing mixture). Snow and salt make a freezing mixture in which the temperature is very much lower than that of the snow by itself.

For real ice-cream, which needs rather expensive ingredients, you had better consult a cookery book. To make fruit-flavoured ices you will need plenty of sugar which you mix with lemonade, fruit juice, or flavourings such as powdered chocolate, coffee or caramel. Milk ices can be prepared by making a kind of pulp with flour, sugar and milk.

Whichever kind you decide to make, prepare it in a small aluminium pan or in a clean tin. Next make your freezing mixture. The coldest freezing mixture consists of three parts of snow to one part of salt. That is, three handfuls or cupfuls of snow to one of salt, well mixed together. Make a layer of the mixture about two inches deep in a large pan, put the small pan on top of this and then keep adding more of the freezing mixture round the sides until only the lid of the small pan is showing.

It takes quite a while before the contents of the small pan are frozen. But you must not let it freeze too much, because then the ice merely gets very hard and does not taste good. Every now and again lift the lid of the pan, and as the contents get nearer to freezing stir them round. If you do not stir sufficiently you will get very large crystals of ice and you will enjoy the ice-cream far less.

60. Make your own clouds and snowstorm
You will need: large tin, small tin, ice or snow, cooking salt.

Some clouds consist of floating ice drops or ice crystals. It often happens on a cold winter's day that small clouds come from your own mouth: the air which you breathe out contains water vapour which condenses to minute droplets. If you would like to study the formation of these little clouds more closely you can make yourself a small refrigerator in which you can produce clouds any time you like.

You can make your own refrigerator by filling a large tin with a mixture of chopped ice or snow and cooking salt – three parts of snow or ice to one part of salt – and putting a smaller tin into it. In the smaller tin the air cools off quite quickly. By blowing into it you introduce water vapour which, because of the low temperature, condenses into tiny drops of water, so forming a small cloud. If you shine a torch into the cold space you will be able to see your cloud more clearly.

If you have a chance of getting some 'dry ice' – solid carbon dioxide which has a temperature many degrees below zero – you can shave a few tiny fragments off it and let them fall into the tin. (Wear thick gloves when you hold the dry ice.) Then you will see the minute drops of water change into thousands of tiny floating crystals of ice. With your torch and a magnifying glass you can get a wonderful view of what happens. Keep on blowing very carefully into the cloud, and more and more floating ice crystals will keep forming and eventually fall to the bottom of the tin like a cloud of snow.

61. Soap bubbles of . . . crystal

You will need: soapy water or one of the special bubble solutions, clay pipe or a piece of wire, nice sharp frost, some sugar.

Soap bubbles of crystal – can it be true? Yes, certainly. You can have them by letting soap bubbles freeze. That's delightful – like a fairytale. But, to make it work, there must be a really sharp frost outside and practically no wind.

Make a really good soap solution with warm water and stir some sugar into it – that makes the strongest bubbles. Let it stand outside until it has got ice-cold. Instead of the soap solution you can use one of these 'wonder bubble mixtures' which you can buy so cheaply nowadays from nearly all toyshops. It makes beautifully large and strong bubbles.

How do you blow big bubbles? One way is with a clay pipe, but you can do even better with a wire ring which you can make quite easily for yourself. The ring must be perfectly round – so bend the wire round some circular object. Dip the ring vertically into the liquid and lift it out carefully – across the ring is a thin film of soap solution – and then blow gently. With reasonable luck you will get a fine big bubble.

But don't let the bubble fly off. Hold it up carefully by the ring or the pipe. Because the liquid is already very cold and the film is so thin, it soon freezes. By watching closely you can actually follow the freezing of the bubble. In the lovely colours which make bubbles so fairylike you can see tiny stars and other crystalline shapes moving over the curved surface of the bubble until it freezes completely.

So, you have obtained an ice-crystal ball, a ball with

a thickness of less than a thousandth of an inch. If you can catch one of these frozen bubbles on a cold dry cloth it will stay there for quite a considerable time and you can study it at your leisure. If the sun is shining you can see the crystals which make up your cobweb ball glistening and shining like diamonds. . . .

62. Right through the ice, but the ice stays whole

You will need: block of ice, 2 boxes, thin wire, heavy weight, pair of wire-cutters, needle.

If you fall through the ice, the ice does not stay in one piece and you get your clothes wet. But a very thin wire can do what you cannot do – go through the ice without making a hole. Take a block of ice and lay it across two boxes or other supports. You can make yourself a suitable block of ice by filling a rectangular plastic box with water and leaving it in the refrigerator, or use the usual box for making small blocks but take the separators out. In the latter case it is better to make two similar blocks, wet each of them on one face, sprinkle some salt over them and then press the two wet faces together. Then they will fuse together into one piece.

Fasten a string to a large stone, an old flat-iron or some similar heavy weight, lay a thin wire (copper wire is best) over your block of ice and fasten the two

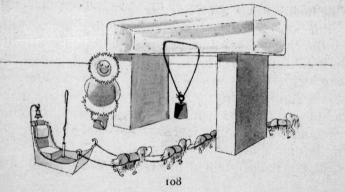

ends of the wire to the string on the weight. Make sure that the weight can hang free without touching the ground.

You will see the wire slowly cut through the ice – pulled down by the weight – but to your surprise you will see that the ice above the wire remains in one piece. In the end the wire cuts right through the block of ice, but it is still in one piece.

How is this possible? Because of the pressure of the wire the melting point of the ice is lowered, so that immediately below the wire the ice melts. But immediately above the wire there is no pressure, and so the water freezes again. You can also see this if you use a nail. Grip it firmly in a pair of pliers and press it firmly against a piece of ice. The nail goes right into the ice without breaking it, and it may even be possible to push the nail all the way through without leaving a hole in the ice.

It has been suggested that skating depends on the melting of the ice below the skates by the lowering of the melting point caused by the pressure. But this is not so unless the ice is almost at its melting point already. The pressure beneath the narrow blade produced by the weight of the heaviest skater is not sufficient to lower the melting point below $-0.75°C$. So, as the ice is usually already well below this temperature, the pressure has no effect. Skating, sleighing and skiing are possible because of the low friction between polished steel and ice.

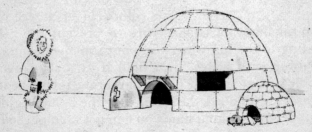

If you squeeze some fresh snow, or snow which is beginning to melt, the pressure on the sharp corners of the crystals is sufficient to cause them to melt. Then, when the pressure is released, the flakes freeze again and stick together – hence snowballs. You have probably found that if it is very cold it is very difficult to make snowballs: the snowflakes will not stick together. Now you know why.

The formation of glaciers is explained by the pressure exerted by the great weight of the layers of snow. Because of the weight above, the lower layers lose their beautiful crystalline shapes and become packed into hard ice. The slow movement over the rocks is assisted by the weight of the hundred-foot-thick glacier melting the bottom layer, the melted water forming an excellent lubricant.

63. Does ice melt in boiling water?

You will need: test tube, some pieces of ice, thin copper wire, candle.

What a silly question isn't it? Of course ice melts in boiling water. Unless . . . yes, unless it *doesn't* melt. Let's try it. In the bottom of a test tube, or one of those glass tubes in which tablets are sometimes sold, put one or two small pieces of ice. Over the ice push a spiral made of copper wire to prevent the pieces floating to the top when you pour some water in. Fill the tube with water, then hold it at a slant over a candle so that only the upper part of the tube is heated. After a few minutes the water over the flame begins to boil, yet at the same time you can get hold of the bottom of the tube without burning yourself, and the ice at the bottom does not melt.

How does it happen? Water is a poor conductor of heat. Although part of the water in the tube is boiling, the rest stays cold. Circulation does not take place because cold water is denser than hot and so remains at the bottom.

Because water is such a poor conductor of heat, even in the warmest oceans around the equator, the water deep down remains cold. Consequently it is advisable, when swimming in these seas, to remain on the surface and not to swim several thousands of feet down. You could so easily catch cold!

64. Make a steam turbine

You will need: tin can, some tinplate (this can be cut from an old tin), 2 small nuts and bolts, with 4 rubber washers, tools (scissors, pliers).

The steam engine with cylinders and pistons has largely been replaced by the steam turbine, and enormous engines of this type can be found in power stations and in ships. We can easily make a real steam turbine ourselves.

Cut a perfectly round disc from a piece of tinplate with a pair of old scissors, or better still, with tin shears. The disc should be about 2½ inches diameter.

Make cuts inwards, along radii, of about $\frac{1}{2}$ inch, and with a pair of pliers twist the bits of tin, all in the same direction. In this way you will obtain a paddle wheel.

Bend a long strip of tinplate as shown in the drawing, bore four holes in it, two for the axle of the paddle wheel and two for the small bolts which are going to fasten the strip to the lid of the tin. Bore two holes in the lid also for these bolts, and make a third hole through which the steam will be able to escape and shoot up against your wheel. Make sure that you put a couple of rubber or plastic washers between the nuts and the lid before you fasten them up tight. These will prevent the steam from escaping from the wrong places. You can use a long nail for the axle of your paddle wheel, and the wheel can be made secure on it with two corks. Your turbine is now complete.

Fill the can to one third with water, put the lid on firmly and stand the tin over the gas on the stove or on the hotplate of the cooker.

When the water boils, a jet of steam shoots out of the hole in the lid and your turbine starts to spin round at high speed. If the lid is not 'steam-tight', cut a wide washer of thin plastic and lay it over the edge of the can before you put the lid on. Use a little grease or oil on the bearings; if they are carefully made the turbine will get up to a really high speed.

65. Pick the right coin every time
You will need: some large coins, hat.

Many conjuring tricks depend upon subtle applications of scientific principles. This also applies to the following trick. Get a group of people to put together a number of similar coins, e.g. pennies. Somebody chooses one of them, takes careful note of the date or some other identifying mark, and then it is passed from hand to hand. Everybody must hold the coin in the palm of his hand, and grasp it firmly while thinking hard about it. When all have done it the coin is returned to the hat. Then someone who has not been watching what has been going on (either because he has had his back to the company, or because he has been outside the room) picks out the coin purely by feel, without looking.

The one who wants to pass himself off as a real magician must look as though he is concentrating deeply and is trying to read the thoughts of the company, but all that he really has to do is to touch the different coins lightly and to feel which of the coins is warm. The rest of them will be at room temperature, but the coin which has been held in everybody's hand will be warmer and easy to pick out.

It is interesting, when you are watching a performance by a conjurer, magician or whatever he calls himself, to try to work out how far he uses scientific principles in his tricks, and what they are. A lot depends on quickness of the hand, bluff, and subtle misleading of the audience but science is the magician's chief accomplice.

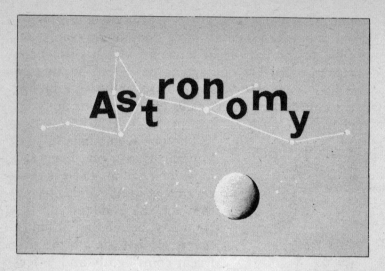

Astronomy

66. Between you and infinity there are billions of stars

There was a time when men stared longingly at the white patches on the globe and were fascinated by the challenging words 'terra incognita'. The longing led to action; all the land was explored, all the seas were charted; the eternal silence of the poles was broken and now we live in a world almost without secrets.

But the kingdom of the moon and the planets, the sun and the stars, arches magnificently and mysteriously over us. There lies untrodden territory, and the men of science use their mighty telescopes to search the heavens and wrest one secret after another from them. Now that man has walked on the moon they eagerly await the day when space travel will enable them to explore Mars and perhaps other planets.

Such journeys of exploration are within the realms of possibility for them, but will they ever succeed in leaving our solar system and reaching other solar systems? For even if one moved at the greatest speed possible (which, according to Professor Einstein, is 186,000 miles per second, the speed of light, radio and other electromagnetic waves) it would take five years to reach the nearest star. Such a star – an unimaginably hot ball of gas – is not an attractive destination, but it is probable that planets circle round many stars like it and, who knows, perhaps there are some like our earth. . . .

To the moon and the sun on a ray of light

If one could travel through space at the speed of light, then very shortly after leaving the earth, we should land on the moon, which is only 235,000 miles away from us. . . .

We should find ourselves standing on a rocky ridge covered with a thick layer of dust in the middle of a horrible, dead landscape. Before us stretches a barren plain, also covered with dust, scarred by deep craters, long, yawning chasms, with high mountains of dirty white rock in the background. No breath of wind, not even the smallest sound, breaks the silence of this waste; there is no blade of grass, not even the smallest insect – not a sign of life anywhere. The blazing sun beats scorchingly down on the white-hot masses of rock, the blindingly bright and fantastically shaped mountains are in striking contrast to the jet-black sky. . . .

Is this the moon, the good friend of our childhood days with his beaming face and his fairylike glow? How warm and flourishing our earth is in comparison,

with her abundance of plants and animals, seas and clouds, colours, light and life!

The earth! She hangs above the horizon like an enormous, delicately coloured Chinese lantern, a large unreal variegated saucer-with-a-bite-out-of-it, shining brightly against the black of the sky in which the stars burn fiercely and fixedly. The earth lives, but the moon is dead, without water and without air, murderously hot for two weeks, and then more than 100°C below freezing point for two weeks! Brrr, how cold! It's about time we had a look on the sunny side of things. We set course for the sun at full speed ahead, 186,000 miles per second, and arrive after 8 minutes. The first thing we look for is an ice-cream parlour. . . .

No, that's a feeble joke, because not even a ton of ice-cream could refresh us here. The sun is a white-hot ball of gas, more than a million times as big as the earth, with a surface temperature of 6,000°C and a temperature at its centre of more than 10 million degrees, with a pressure of thousands of millions of atmospheres!

Everything is big on the sun. If the sun is troubled by freckles, which seen through smoked glass look like minute little spots, then each freckle is larger than the earth. Each one of these insignificant sun spots is an enormous cyclone of hot gases which sends out masses of electrically charged particles. These are the cause of all sorts of mysterious phenomena on our earth 93 million miles away; telegraph and wireless communications are interrupted, magnetic storms arise, bright northern lights with their strange shapes and colours appear, yes, even rainfall and plant life are affected by them.

Everything is big on the sun. From time to time the sun puts its tongue out – that is to say, there is a gigantic gas explosion which shoots out hundreds of thousands of miles in a few hours. It's a pity that 'protuberances' like this can only be seen when there's a total eclipse of the sun, and this happens relatively so seldom that scientists organize large-scale expeditions and travel thousands of miles to be able to observe it.

Mars – minus Martians

But talking of travelling, we are going further on our ray of light. We have set course for Mars! Mars, the red planet. Mars, with its canals and Martians! However many people were there who believed in that at the end of the last century? Through telescopes they saw white patches at the poles of Mars with blue belts around them and there were also red and yellow plains which sometimes turned green and were intersected by a number of vague, straight lines. People concluded from this that there were ice-caps and deserts, which were sometimes covered with plant life, while human fancy made the blue belts and the vague, straight lines into seas and . . . canals. Becoming more fanciful, they concluded that these canals could only have been dug by civilized human beings.

This news was exaggeratedly reported by the Press and was a sensation for the newspaper readers. Mars was inhabited by people who, judging by their vast system of canals, must have a much more advanced civilization than even the inhabitants of the earth! The name Mars was on many a tongue, plans were made for contacting the Martians by means of light signals and later by wireless, people indulged in fanciful dreams and many were filled with a terrific enthusiasm until. . . .

Until the scientists, most of whom had kept a cool head, brought all these castles in the air tumbling down. Further investigation proved that the canals were an optical illusion and in fact were rows of small spots. There could also be no possibility of human life like ours because of the almost entire lack of water and oxygen. But all the same the chance of life on Mars, the diameter of which is half that of the earth, is greater than on the other planets. There is a rarefied atmosphere, the temperature at its equator varies from $-40°C$ to $+25°C$ and because of the seasonal appearance of a green tint, it is thought possible that there are lower forms of life such as lichen and algae.

Meanwhile with all this talk about Mars, we have rushed right past it. But never mind, because there's a new apparition already, the ghost of the land of stars, a round patch of light with a huge tail. The patch visibly swells and its tail grows into an enormous white sweep covering a large area of the sky with a gossamer and luminous veil. We fly towards the ghost at an alarming speed . . . a crash, a crash shattering everything cannot be avoided. Paralysed with fear we await our end. The patch has swollen into a luminous cloud of bewildering size, a mysterious, silvery radiance surrounds us, we dive into a sea of milky white light as if in a submarine and then . . . all that light dissolves in the inky black sky and disappears! We've rushed headlong through the tail of a comet, more than a hundred million miles long, and nothing has happened to us. . . .

Dwarfs and giants

Now we see something else strange, an immensely long procession of colossal boulders rushing by one after the other. They are planetoids, possibly the fragments of an exploded planet. They circle the sun like a tribe of dwarfs. Imagine that you live on a miniature heavenly body like this. It is the same size as London for example, and travels through space like a gigantic mountain lifted off its pedestal. One could walk round it in a few days without falling off. The force of gravity is much less here than on earth and therefore the heaviest of us weighs no more than a matchstick and the weakest can easily pick up a steam engine. But we mustn't get too excited as one high jump into the air would shoot us immediately into space, and we would be doomed to circle eternally round the sun as an independent heavenly body, a human planetoid.

On our ray of light we leave the dwarfs and travel towards a giant nearly a thousand times as big as the earth. In the distance we see a colossal ball surrounded by a set of flat rings which brightly reflect the sunlight. It is Saturn and his rings!

There is a thick layer of methane and ammonia clouds, so unfortunately we can't see its vast surface. Saturn is surrounded by an armour of ice thousands of miles thick. If it wasn't so cold and cloudy, lovers of moonlight idylls could enjoy themselves there to their hearts' content. Saturn has ten moons! What would add most to the romantic atmosphere, however, would be the rings. These bridge the black, diamond-studded heaven like a mighty bow of dull silver. The rings consist of small particles the size of a grain of sand. Perhaps they are the pieces of an exploded Saturn moon and it is conceivable that our own moon will undergo the same fate in the distant future. Then, after a heavy meteor bombardment, the earth would also be surrounded by a splendidly glittering ring of light.

To eternity via the Milky Way

We travel fast through the solar system, right through that vast space in which the earth and her eight sisters, the planets Mercury, Venus, Mars, Jupiter – the biggest, Saturn, Uranus, Neptune and Pluto move in elliptical orbits round the sun, and we penetrate deeper into the universe. The universe is so empty that if we reduce all the measurements and distances a million times, then the stars, which have shrunk to the size of pinheads, are still on an average 100 miles apart. There are a dozen pinheads in a region as large as England. That's how sparsely the stars are scattered. . . .

We find that out for ourselves as we travel on and on, day after day, night after night, at a steady speed of 186,000 miles per second without meeting a single star. The solar system is far behind us, the sun is just a twinkling star, the earth is invisible, not even a pinpoint of light betrays its presence. The months turn into years before we reach the nearest star. Yet more years pass before we reach the next star. And so it goes on, from star to star, on and on for centuries; at ever the same speed we cleave through the universe of the stars – stars of all sorts and sizes, blue, white, yellow, orange, pink and red, all fiery balls of gas, some hotter, some cooler, dwarfs and giants. Giants a million times as big as the sun, which in its turn is a million times bigger than the earth. Dwarfs, white dwarfs, the substance of which is so tightly packed and pressed together that a matchbox full of it on earth would weigh many tons!

We rush on without rest for hundreds, thousands, tens of thousands of years, we shoot past yet more stars, those gigantic, fiery balls of gas, many of which are probably surrounded by planetary systems, we fly through countless swarms of stars. Then we leave the star system which includes all the stars we can see from the earth and has a diameter of approximately 100,000 light years. A light year is the distance light travels in a year, 6,000,000,000,000 miles. We leave the lens-shaped Milky Way, in which the earth is as insignificant as a drop of water in the ocean. . . .

Now there is an even greater void, the hundred thousand years through which we shoot at a speed of 186,000 miles per second. But that doesn't mean the end of the stars in the universe. Dim patches of light swell up into new islands of the universe, into new and mighty astral systems full of a blinding splendour such as the Andromeda nebula, more than 2 million light years away from the earth.

And so we hurry on, for millions of years, on and on; on through innumerable multitudes of shining stars, on, on and on, on into the immeasurable depths of the universe, in which space and time flow together into timeless infinity, and our thoughts, filled with admiration for the mystery of creation, melt into dreamless, eternal sleep. . . .

67. Make a model of the expanding universe

You will need: inflatable balloon, paintbrush, bottle of ink or paint.

From the observations of the astronomers it appears that the many millions of star systems like the Milky Way, each consisting of thousands of millions of stars, are moving away from each other – as though they were fleeing from each other. All these star systems together form the Universe. Because the systems, or galaxies, are all the time moving further and further apart the Universe is continually expanding. So we come to talk about 'the expanding universe'.

You can make quite a good imitation of this expanding universe by inflating a balloon slightly and then marking spots on it with a watercolour brush dipped in ink or paint. Each spot can stand for a galaxy. Now blow the balloon up; it swells, and the spots on the expanding surface of the balloon move further away from each other. Scientists believe that the galaxies are arranged as if on a surface like the balloon's, with no actual 'centre', and that they move apart in a similar way.

It is not known if this expansion of the universe will continue. Perhaps after some time it contracts and then later expands again: the pulsating universe. You can imitate this, too, with your model by holding the inflated balloon in your mouth and alternately breathing in and out.

68. A spiral nebula from . . . tea-leaves

You will need: pan or dish with a flat bottom, some used tea leaves, water, spoon.

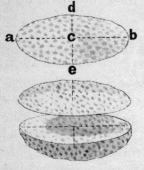

Look at the sky on a clear, moonless night, preferably when no street lights are on. You will see that the stars are not spread out evenly all over the sky. They occur most frequently in a curved streak which teems with stars and is called the Milky Way. What is the explanation?

Our sun, together with thousands of millions of stars, form a crowd of stars in the form of a double convex lens. Or, to use another example, the shape of a currant bun. Imagine that the currants are distributed evenly throughout the bun, and that the bun itself is transparent. Then a person who could get inside the bun and look outwards would see far more currants in the direction *ca* or *cb* than in the directions of *cd* or *ce*. In an arc from *a* to *b*, perpendicular to the surface *adbe*, he will see a great number of currants; in the other direction, *cd*, far fewer.

We earth dwellers really are 'inside the bun'. Looking along the longer axis of the star cluster, we see a great number of stars; and along the short axis we are looking through a much thinner layer and thus through far fewer stars. This very roughly explains the Milky Way.

This lens-shaped star cluster, of which our Solar System forms a part, is our Milky Way system. But there are millions of other systems like our Milky Way, each consisting of millions of stars. With the aid of very strong telescopes it has been observed that many of these systems have a spiral shape. They are called spiral nebulae. Spiral nebulae consist of light and dark clouds as well as millions of stars. Our own Milky Way is one of these spiral nebulae.

We can imitate very nicely the shape of such a spiral nebula in an ordinary pan of water, preferably a pan with a white bottom. Instead of stars we can use . . . tea-leaves!

Put some used tea-leaves into a flat-bottomed pan about three quarters full of water. Give the water a brisk stir with the spoon, then remove the spoon and pay close attention to what takes place. As the motion of the water slows down, the tea-leaves move in spiral paths towards the centre of the pan, giving a picture looking very like the photographs of spiral nebulae taken by the biggest telescopes in the world.

69. Make your own eclipse of the sun and moon

You will need: electric lamp in a well insulated holder, some wire, very small ball – the smallest you can get, table tennis ball, some sticky tape.

In ancient times people were terrified by an eclipse of the sun or moon and they thought that some great disaster was going to take place. We know better and understand how these phenomena occur. An eclipse of the sun is caused by the moon coming between us and the sun so that we cannot see the sun. In an eclipse of the moon the earth passes between the moon and the sun so that the shadow of the earth falls upon the moon. We can imitate both of these events with a home-made sun, earth and moon.

Shall we use an electric lamp for our sun? It will do,

provided that it is in a well-insulated holder so that there is not the slightest chance of your getting a dangerous shock. We could make our earth and moon from clay or some similar material, carefully moulded into small balls. The diameters of sun, earth and moon are in the ratios $100:1:\frac{1}{4}$, but if we were to adhere strictly to these proportions the earth would have to be no bigger than a pin's head. For the earth, therefore, use a table tennis ball and for the moon as small a ball as you can get. In order to let the earth rotate round the sun, and the moon round the earth (as in fact, they do) we must fasten them together by means of stiff wires as shown in the drawing. The longest wire must be wound closely round the lampholder, the shortest round the wire immediately below the earth. Fasten the earth and the moon to the ends of their wires with transparent adhesive tape.

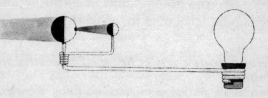

In the drawing above you see how an eclipse of the sun takes place. You must turn the balls round until the moon comes between the sun and the earth and they are all in one straight line. This is what actually happens. You can see the shadow of the moon falling on the earth. But this does not mean that no light at all falls on the earth. A total eclipse only takes place at a very small part of the earth's surface, just that small area on which the moon's shadow falls.

Now turn the moon until the earth comes between the sun and the moon, and all three are in a straight line again. Now we have a demonstration of an eclipse of the moon. If only the lamp is alight and the rest of the room is dark you will see that no light falls on the moon at all: it stays completely dark.

Back to the eclipse of the sun again. If you hold your eye close to the earth, and move the moon into different positions you will be able to observe the different phases of the moon; the crescent moon and the half moon show up clearly and you can follow how they are caused. If you want to improve your model you can paint some of the parts.

70. Make an astronomical telescope

You will need: 2 cardboard tubes to fit one inside the other, spectacle lens with a focal length of 50cm, strong magnifying glass, focal length 2cm, some wood, wire, paste or gum, dead black paint, cardboard.

It is possible to make a reasonably good telescope with quite simple materials. You start with two cardboard tubes such as those used for sending drawings and maps through the post. They must fit snugly together. If necessary make the smaller tube wide enough by pasting an extra layer or two of thin paper round it. It is essential to paint the insides of the tubes with dead black paint. Blackboard paint will do very well.

For the objective lens you can use a plano-convex, or double convex lens with a focal length of about 50 centimetres. You can measure the focal length by using your lens as a burning glass in the sunshine. All you have to do is measure the distance between the lens and the charred spot on the paper. The focal length can be a little greater than 50 centimetres. If you have to buy a lens, ask for a spectacle lens of 50 centimetres focal length (+2 dioptres).

The eyepiece from a microscope or from a binocular will do excellently as an eyepiece for your telescope. Or you can use a very strong magnifying glass or one of the 'linen testers' used in the textile industry; the focal length should be in the region of 2 centimetres. You can calculate the magnification of your telescope by dividing the smaller focal length into the larger, e.g. 50 cm ÷ 2cm = 25. So, the telescope magnifies 25 times.

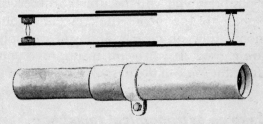

Fix the large lens into one of the tubes with a couple of cardboard or wooden rings glued in, or make rings from wire. Mount the eyepiece in a wooden spool with a hole in it. It is most important that the two lenses lie on the same axis and that they are mounted square in the cardboard tubes. The telescope gives an inverted image, but for astronomical observations that does not matter. The edges of the images will be coloured slightly. This can be reduced quite a lot by putting in front of the objective lens a diaphragm, a piece of tin or card with a hole of $1\frac{1}{2}$ inches diameter in it.

Of course the telescope can be made stouter and stronger, for instance by using metal tubes and stronger lenses. An objective lens of 100 centimetres focal length and an eyepiece of 2 centimetres give a magnification of 50 times.

It is almost impossible to see well with the telescope

if you hold it in your hand. To get a completely motionless image, sharp and clear by sliding the tubes in and out, it is essential to have a firm support for the telescope. Anyone who is reasonably good at woodwork can soon make a steady support for it. Round the telescope fasten a ring of tinplate – it can be held firmly with a wingnut. Kitchen steps, or even a chair, will make a passable support. If you are a handyman you may be able to work out some ideas of your own.

Lenses can often be obtained in shops dealing in surplus government equipment.

71. Bring the moon, planets and stars nearer
You will need: telescope.

Even with a simple pair of opera glasses you can see more in the night sky than you can with the naked eye. And an ordinary pair of 8 × binoculars makes a very powerful vehicle for voyages of discovery through the heavens. Under the most favourable conditions only a few thousand stars are visible to the unaided eye, but a pair of prism binoculars reveals more than a hundred thousand! But with a telescope which magnifies 25 to 50 times you are able to observe particularly interesting details of the moon and some of the planets.

The most interesting target is the moon, which is at its most beautiful at the last or first quarter. Then the sunlight falls upon the moon at a slant, throwing shadows of the mountains and enabling you to see the craters at their best. At full moon the sunlight falls full upon the moon and it is not so interesting to observe. If you look carefully you can see, in the boundary between the sunlight and the dark on the moon, white spots which lie in the dark area. They are the peaks of high mountains, still lit up by sunlight, while all the surrounding lower land is still in darkness. Take a good look at the moon, for at least a quarter of an hour, for as many successive evenings as you can. Then you will see more and more details every evening.

With sufficient magnification you see the planets as discs; stars remain as points of light, even with the largest reflecting telescope in the world – such as the Mount Palomar telescope in the U.S.A. with a diameter of over sixteen feet and a magnification of 10,000. The biggest and brightest planet in the night sky is Jupiter. With binoculars you can see quite clearly, four bright spots on one side or the other of the planet, lying almost in a straight line. They are four of Jupiter's twelve moons. Look there again on successive evenings – each evening they are in a different position.

With ordinary binoculars you can see that there is something unusual about the planet Saturn, but only with a stronger telescope is it possible to see that the planet is surrounded by a ring – a very thrilling spectacle. The planet Venus, which you can find in the direction of the sunrise or sunset, has phases just like the moon so that it often has the crescent shape which is visible with a stronger telescope. The planet

Mars, recognizable by its red colour, is rather disappointing. But with a strong telescope and under favourable conditions you can see something spotted or a trace of the white pole caps.

Of course you can see the stars and planets best on a moonless night with a clear sky from a position where there are no street lamps. Point your binoculars towards the Milky Way and then you will really see innumerable stars. In order to be able to find certain stars and star patterns, or constellations, you will have to get a star guide or star chart. With the help of the chart aim your telescope towards the places where stars are clustered close together, as in the Pleiades, the Crab, Taurus, Dolphin; look at the nebula in Orion, a mighty gas cloud in which, over perhaps millions of years, new stars are formed; and look at the Andromeda nebula, which is not a nebula but a Milky Way or galaxy of thousands of millions of stars far beyond our own galaxy. While you are looking towards the Andromeda nebula just think that the rays of light from it, in spite of their enormous speed of 186,000 miles a second, have taken over 900,000 years to reach the earth. So you are seeing that galaxy as it was 900,000 years ago!

72. See sunspots

You will need: telescope, very dark negative or very dark piece of smoked glass, some adhesive tape.

It is very dangerous indeed to look directly at the sun. You can get very serious inflammation of the eye; you can even go blind. If you look straight at the sun with a telescope the danger is even greater. So, never, never do it!

If you want to look at the sun you must look through a *very* dark photographic negative, a *very* dark piece of glass or a piece of glass which you have covered with soot by holding it over the flame from a wad of cotton wool soaked in turpentine or over a smoky oil lamp. Then you will see the sun as a yellow disc, and perhaps you will observe one or two tiny specks on it. They ... are sunspots!

Sunspots are cooler spots on the surface of the glowing ball of gas which give out less light than their surroundings and therefore appear darker. These sunspots can be larger than the whole earth and the vehemence with which the cooler gases stream through the hotter ones and the giant hurricanes or whirlwinds which are caused make the imagination boggle. Some of the spots last for just a few days, others for weeks or even for months.

The very largest sunspots are visible to the naked eye through a smoked glass, but to see the small ones, which occur far more frequently you need a telescope. If you can get a pair of opera glasses or prismatic binoculars, fasten over each of the objective lenses a *very* dark negative with some adhesive tape. Then, if you look very carefully there is a good chance that you will see some of these famous sunspots.

If you have a telescope with even greater magnification you can fasten the dark negative or smoked glass in front of the objective or behind the eyepiece or through a slot in the side of the tube. With a magnification of some tens of times you can often see whole clusters of large and small sunspots. If you find a good cluster of spots repeat your observations every few hours and every few days. Sunspots can move; moreover the sun turns around its axis in rather less than four weeks.

With a telescope it is possible to project an image of the sun's disc on to a piece of paper; with ordinary prism binoculars the result can be outstanding. Of course you will have to remove the smoked glass. By keeping the surroundings as dark as possible – drawing the curtains, for instance – you can see the sunspots quite clearly on the projected image and you can trace round them with a pencil. By using the same method astronomers draw the sunspots every day and measure their sizes. You can see the projected image even more sharply and clearly by looking at it through a magnifying glass.

73. Make a sundial
You will need: knitting needle, piece of stiff white card, pencil, cork.

Cut out from the piece of white card a circle through the centre of which you push the knitting needle. You have already pushed the needle through the cork to make a support for the disc. Now stick the needle upright into the ground.

Ask the sun to shine for you, for the whole thing depends on its shadow. Where the shadow falls at 12 o'clock make a mark on the card and label it 12. Where the shadow falls at 1 o'clock, make another mark with 1 beside it. Do the same at every hour from sunrise to sunset. Then you will have made a clock, which is quite reliable while the sun shines.

Of course there are many other ways of making a sundial, for example with a small board and a metal rod. Or with a stick and a 'dial' marked out with stones or flowers. The second picture shows you how you can fix up a sundial with a vertical scale on a south-facing wall.

74. Where is the south?

You will need: watch.

There are several ways of finding the points of the compass and so discovering where the north or the south is. If you know that, it is a simple matter to work out where east and west are.

How do you find the north? A compass is the best-known method. A magnetized needle or magnetized razor blade floating in a cup of water forms a very serviceable compass. But if you have no compass, magnetic needle or razor blade with you? For somebody who knows how to find the Pole Star on a clear starry night it is not difficult. The Pole Star is always at the north. But in daytime . . . ?

At twelve noon the sun stands exactly in the south. At that moment it is quite easy to find the south and north. But at other times too it is possible to find the south and the north and hence the east and the west. And you can do it with the help of a watch.

Lay the watch down so that the small hand points exactly towards the sun. Bisect the angle between the small hand and 12 – see the drawing – and this bisector, the arrow in the drawing, points to the south. Suppose you are on holiday, making your way with the aid of a map, or you have got lost, it is very useful if you can find the south and the other points of the compass. Lay the map under the watch so that the bisector points straight towards the lower edge of the map.

75. Foucault's pendulum

You will need: plate, cork, 3 forks, apple, 2 needles, length of thread, some fine salt.

In the year 1851 the French scientist Foucault demonstrated a spectacular proof of the rotation of the earth. Under the famous dome of the Pantheon in Paris he let a heavy pendulum make grooves in some sand on the floor. While the pendulum, like every free hanging pendulum, continues to swing in the same direction in the same plane, the earth, and the floor of the Pantheon, rotated below it. Because of this, grooves were made very gradually in other directions in the sand, a demonstration which made Foucault world-famous. In some Science Museums, and certainly in the one in London, you can see a pendulum like Foucault's in action.

We can copy his demonstration on a small scale. We can make the dome of the Pantheon with three forks stuck into a cork and can use a plate for the floor. For our pendulum we can make use of an apple and a piece of thread. Push a needle right through the apple and another right through the cork. Through the two eyes thread some strong thread of just the right length to permit the needle sticking through the apple to barely touch the plate. Sprinkle some fine salt on the plate which represents a part of the earth's surface. Now your Pantheon is complete.

Start the pendulum swinging, and the point of the needle under the apple makes grooves in the salt. Turn the plate round very carefully while the pendulum is swinging and you will see new grooves gradually being made. This shows us, experimentally, that the pendulum continues to swing in the same plane and that it does not follow the rotation of the plate. We have not shown that the earth is rotating by this experiment, but we have repeated Foucault's famous experiment on a small scale in which we have replaced the rotating earth by the rotating plate.

76. The spinning earth

You will need: round pan or basin, water, powdered cork, large piece of card, grater, pair of scissors or a knife.

Were you disappointed that we did not actually demonstrate the rotation of the earth with our previous experiment? Cheer up, for here comes another experiment by which you can make the rotation really visible. Place a circular bowl filled with water on some place free from vibration, for instance a stone floor or dresser. Hold above the water a piece of card out of which you have cut a narrow slot an inch or two shorter than the diameter of the bowl. Right over this slot in the card file or rasp some powder from a cork. Some of the powder will fall through the slot on to the water so that a narrow line of cork-dust floats on the water. The water must be quite still while you are shaking the cork dust over the slot.

Do not touch the bowl and make sure that it remains undisturbed for several hours and if you come back to look at it after, say two or three hours you will see that the cork line has rotated through about 45°. But that is only what seems to have happened, for in fact the line has stayed stationary and the earth and bowl have rotated beneath it. And here you have a really visible demonstration of the rotation of the earth!

Every twenty-four hours the earth turns round once

on its axis, that is through an angle of 360°. So in one hour it turns through $\frac{360°}{24}$, that is, 15°; or one quarter of a degree per second. From this it is obvious that if you found yourself thousands of miles out in space you would not see the earth spinning round in the way often shown in the poorer popular science films. The earth rotates twice as slowly as the small hand of a clock or watch, and you cannot see that move.

Nevertheless, the speed of anyone who lives on the equator is 25,000 ÷ 24, or just over 1,000 miles an hour – faster than sound! But even if you live in higher latitudes you will realize that you can be moving with a speed of 600 miles an hour on this super-roundabout – the earth.

With a strong telescope which magnifies some tens of times it is possible to see the rotation of the earth. Look at any one star and you will see it move slowly across your field of view from east to west. As this happens with other stars too, the movement obviously comes from the motion of the earth.

A letter from the author

Dear Reader,

To me, life is a voyage of exploration full of the
pleasure of discovery. I write my books in the hope of
sharing some of that pleasure with other people - and
especially with young people.

There's another reason, too, why I write about
science: I believe in science as a means of promoting
world prosperity and peace. Two-thirds of the earth's
population is undernourished, millions of people suffer
from painful diseases and every day thousands of
children die through lack of medical care. Science,
combined with a spirit of goodwill, can change this -
can raise the health and living standards of whole
nations and thus lessen the political tensions that
lead to war. The scientist with a sense of responsi-
bility can contribute enormously to the building of a
happier and more peaceful world tomorrow.

So there is a great need for scientists, and from
experience I know how often simple experiments done by
young people can lead to a career as a scientist. Many
great men of science, indeed, started in just this kind
of way: their boyhood hobby was the beginning of their
life's work which benefited mankind.

But even for those who don't choose science as a
career, it is of great importance to get some scientific
knowledge based on actual experience, because everyday

life is full of science. Cleaning, washing and cooking, using a radio or record player or TV, taking photographs, making music, travelling by car, train, ship or aeroplane - all these involve practising or using science. You can't understand how these things work (still less can you repair them if they don't!) unless you have a basic knowledge of science. Luckily the schools are teaching science more and more, but there are also plenty of possibilities at home to penetrate into the secrets and mysteries of nature - just as the great scientific pioneers did - by experiments.

As you can see from the next three pages, this book is my 'second helping' of science experiments. The first book has been published in Holland, Germany, Sweden, Finland, Great Britain, Canada, the U.S.A. and Spain. It fills me with happiness to think that hundreds of thousands of readers, young and old, have done the experiments described in it.

It is my sincere wish that these two Books of Experiments will not only give you pleasure, but also open your eyes to the wonder of nature, stimulate you to discover its laws by your own experiments, and contribute to the development of science for the benefit of all the peoples of the world.

Leonard de Vries

The experiments listed and the illustrations reproduced on these last three pages are only a few of those appearing in the 120-odd pages of Leonard de Vries's previous volume:

The Book of Experiments

Invert a glass of water without spilling a drop
An oil-tin crushed by air pressure
How heavy air is
A banana skins itself
Stick two glasses together with air
Lift 20 lb. of books with your breath
Make a pop-gun from a tube and a potato
Make yourself a hot-air balloon
Make yourself a boomerang
A flour bomb as a noisy finale to our air experiments
Make yourself a compass
Make little magnetic boats
Make a cannon from a bottle
Make a jet boat from an egg
Make a glass steam turbine

Two forks as balancing artists on a needle point
The tightrope-dancing bottle
Make a switchback for water drops
A lion's roar out of a box
Make a telephone from old tins
An organ from empty bottles
Make a harmonica from wineglasses
Make a flat-iron guitar
Iron floats on water
Make a boat propelled by soap
How to make a Cartesian diver
Your hand in the water—but it is not wet!
High tension while you comb your hair
Give yourself a high tension of 10,000 volts
Dolls dance by electricity
An electric roundabout

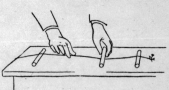

Make yourself an electroscope
A discovery that changed the world
Make an electromagnet
Dance, Miss Paper Clip!
Make a sodium light
Make a Camera Obscura
How to make a kaleidoscope
Electric light from your arm
A magic chemical garden
From sugar to Pharaoh's serpent
Write with invisible ink
The enchanted needles
You have two noses
Make a real steam roundabout
Make an electric motor from nails

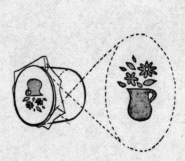